Being Boys, Being Girls:
Learning masculinities
and femininities

Being Boys, Being Girls: Learning masculinities and femininities

Carrie Paechter

Open University Press

Open University Press
McGraw-Hill Education
McGraw-Hill House
Shoppenhangers Road
Maidenhead
Berkshire
England
SL6 2QL

email: enquiries@openup.co.uk
world wide web: www.openup.co.uk

and Two Penn Plaza, New York, NY 10121-2289, USA

First published 2007

A catalogue record of this book is available from the British Library

ISBN-10:   0335 219 748 (pb)   0335 219 756 (hb)
ISBN-13:   9780335219742 (pb)   9780335219759 (hb)

Library of Congress Cataloguing-in-Publication Data
CIP data applied for

Typeset by BookEns Ltd, Royston, Herts.

Printed and bound by CPI Group (UK) Ltd, Croydon, CR0 4YY

The **McGraw·Hill** Companies

For my mother

Contents

Acknowledgements

A number of people have kept me going during the preparation of this book. I would particularly like to thank Debbie Epstein, who encouraged me to explore the theoretical ideas that underpin it, and Christina Hughes, who suggested that I write a book about them. I have also had personal and professional support (often both) from Sheryl Clark, Fin Cullen, Rosalyn George, Paul Golightly, Carolyn Jackson, Janis Jefferies, Barbara Martin, Emma Renold, Lesley Safran Barson and Robert Zimmer. The staff on the second floor of the Business and Intellectual Property Centre at the British Library were unfailingly cheerful and helpful during the term I spent working there. Finally, thanks to Mordecai and Zachary for putting up with living with me through the extended process of writing this.

1 Introduction

It seems strange that all the tuough boys around with faces like wild
baboons started life as babes in prams chiz chiz chiz. i mean you kno
wot weeds babes are they lie about and gurgle and all the lades sa
icky pritty and other uterly wet things.

    Being a baby is alright but soon all the boys who hav been wearing
peticoats chiz chiz chiz begin to get bigger. they start zooming about
like jet fighters climb drane pipes squirt water pisto s make aple pie
beds set booby traps leave tools about the garden refuse to be polite
to visiting aunts run on the flower beds make space rockets out of
pop's golf bag and many other japes and pranks.

(Wilans and Searle 1958: 86)

This book is about how boys and girls learn to be men and women. It is
concerned with how newborn babies become children, teenagers and
then adults, who behave in different ways according to whether they are
male or female. In it, I argue that this process involves learning and
constructing ideas about masculinity and femininity, within the many
social contexts in which people live, and that this is a collective
endeavour, undertaken by and in a myriad of social groups. These
understandings are then incorporated into individual identities, along
with other communally constructed ideas about what different sorts of
people are like. In this book I am therefore developing the idea that
masculinities and femininities are the product of group processes, and
exploring in detail what those processes might be.

    Arguing that ideas about masculinity and femininity and, conse-
quently, ways of being male and female, are communally constructed
within child and adult groups is important for a number of reasons. First,
and most important, it makes it clear that the ways males and females
behave are not simply due to biology; there are variations between them,
but they do not arise straightforwardly from our genetic make-up or from
hormonal influences. Gender differences are, in this model, very much a
social issue. Second, and also of crucial importance, the communal
nature of the construction process gives everyone involved some agency
with respect to what is constructed. Clearly, because power relations are
imbued in social groups and processes, some people will have a stronger
influence than others on the ideas and identities that emerge, but

nevertheless, everyone has a stake. Furthermore, because identity construction is continuous and in a constant state of renegotiation, as power relations change, so will the ways in which masculinities and femininities are constructed: it is a dynamic process. At the same time, however, there will remain a certain degree of inertia in gender relations, because of the continuing presence of those who have a strong stake in particular constructions. This approach to understanding masculinities and femininities also, therefore, helps us to appreciate why social change can sometimes appear to be extraordinarily slow, and how and why gender inequalities are passed from one generation to the next.

Although these processes also take place among groups of adults, in this book I concentrate on how they operate among children. I focus on the process of becoming an adult man or woman, which starts from the moment of birth and continues at least to the end of the teenage years. It seems to me that how children think about themselves, the adults around them and each other, as male and female humans, is fundamental to how they behave. I therefore treat the development of masculine and feminine identities as an essentially cognitive process, arguing that it is children's comprehension both of themselves as male or female, and of what that means in the specific contexts in which they live, that is the driving force behind the differences between how boys and girls behave.

For children in most contemporary societies, there are three key sites in which the communal construction and learning of masculinities and femininities take place: the family; the peer group; and the school. These have different degrees of importance at different times in a child's life. In the very early years, the family is central to a child's developing understanding of what men and women, boys and girls do, and how these activities may differ according to gender. Young children have a strong tendency to generalization, and they will draw conclusions about all males and females from what they see around them in their immediate environment. Consequently, after developing my theoretical framework in Chapters 2 and 3, I turn in Chapter 4 to a discussion of the gendered nature of family life, exploring what a child is likely to experience in her or his immediate home environment and what she or he understands from it.

Following this, in Chapters 5 and 6, I concern myself with institutional settings, and what happens to children from the age of about 3, when many encounter group care or education environments for the first time, up until the age of 11 or 12, when they move to secondary education. Chapter 5 concentrates on early years educational and care settings, where children are usually in a play-based environment in which they can have a considerable degree of interaction with each other, even though the environment is largely structured by adults. This is a crucial stage in children's cognitive understanding of gender, as it is during this period that they gradually come to appreciate that gender is fixed, that if they are a girl they will inexorably and permanently become a woman, if a boy, a man. I explore how this key developmental step is influenced by, and influences, early years settings. This is followed in the next chapter by a consideration of how children's ideas about masculinities and femininities change as they move into the more formal world of the primary classroom. Here I explore how schooling structures, especially the bodily regulation of children in school, support and encourage the construction of particular forms of masculinity and femininity.

Of course, classrooms are not the only places where children construct and enact their ideas about how boys and girls behave: playgrounds are also of enormous importance. In Chapter 7, I look in detail at the social processes that take place in school and community playgrounds, and how we might intervene in these. Drawing on my own research in this area, I consider how children's ideas of masculinity and femininity change as they grow older and start to anticipate adolescence, and what the long-term implications are of the ways in which primary age children play.

I then return to formal educational settings, with a consideration, in Chapter 8, of secondary schooling and how masculinities and femininities are constructed by young people in relation to the school as an institution and a system, and to the school curriculum. I explore how secondary schools take the disciplining of the body even further than those for younger children, and how this affects how young people develop masculine and feminine identities through schooling processes. I focus in particular on the academic curriculum, the implications of the labelling of different subjects as masculine or feminine, and on the strongly gendered and classed nature of practical and vocational curricula, and how this is bound up with issues of social class.

Peer group cultures are especially important in adolescence. In Chapter 9, I consider these in detail, exploring how masculinities and femininities are constructed within different teenage subgroups. During this time, young people undergo an intense exploration of what sort of adults they want to be, and they do this by aligning themselves firmly with specific groups, defining themselves according to who they are not, as much as by who they are. This can lead to strongly differentiated masculinities and femininities related to these groups, with long-term implications for possible adult identities.

Underpinning all of this is the idea that masculinities and femininities are locally constructed by participants in what I have called 'communities of masculinity and femininity practice'. How these operate, and how they are affected by power relations within and between groups, is explained in Chapter 3. Before that, in Chapter 2, I introduce some of the ideas that underlie this book: the legacy of mind/ body dualism; my use of the concepts of masculinity and femininity; the importance of the body; the idea that masculinities and femininities are performed, both to others and to the self; and my understanding of the gendered nature of the relationship between power and knowledge.

How children move from a babyhood in which male and female behaviour is basically the same, to an adulthood in which it is significantly different, is something that it is essential to try to understand. Adult masculinities and femininities are not different but equal: they are imbued with power/knowledge relations which operate, much of the time, to the benefit of specific groups, and which limit the possibilities of both male and female identities. If we are to change this situation we need to have a detailed understanding of how adults come to understand themselves as men and women, and what this means to them. We can do this by examining the processes through which they reach these adult selves. This may give us the tools to intervene and construct a more just and equal society, in which the ways that people can be are less constricted than they are now.

2 Sex and gender, power and knowledge

She looked back down her years at school, the reined-in feeling, the stupors of boredom, the teachers in the classrooms like tired lion-tamers, and felt quite the opposite. She was about to be let out. And every day when she left the house, there was the excitement of being noticed, the warmth of eye-beams, the unfolding consciousness of her own attractive powers. She was the focus of every film she saw, every novel she read. She was about to start careering round like a lustrous loose cannon ...

She would never be like her mother, making rotas and lists and endless arrangements, lost forever in a forest of twitching detail with her tense talk of juggling and her self-importance about her precious job and her joyless 'running the family'. No, life was not some sort of military campaign; or, at least, *hers* would not be.

(Simpson 2001b: 2–3)

Introduction

It is easy to understand why one of the elementary forms of political power should have consisted, in many archaic societies, in the almost magical power of *naming* and bringing into existence by virtue of naming.

(Bourdieu 1991: 236)

When a baby is born, almost the first thing that people want to know is what sex it is. Once the child has been seen to be healthy, this is the next thing that is ascertained and announced. Divisions between male and female, masculine and feminine, are fundamental to the operation of most contemporary societies, and so it is essential that a baby is categorized, assigned to one sex or another, as early as possible. This book is about what happens next. My purpose is to answer the question: from the point at which the baby's sex is named, what are the processes by which girls and boys come to understand these aspects of their identities, to construct and to claim them, and to project their constructions to others?

When we assign a sex to a baby, that is when we name the baby's sex, we perform an act which places the baby into a clear category from which we then expect to make predictions about its future. This performative act of naming (Bourdieu 1991) is extraordinarily powerful: it is a crucial point in the child's life which assigns, in most cases for ever, a major social category to which the child is now considered to belong. The distinction between male and female is fundamental to how we understand ourselves as human beings. It governs how individuals are treated, roles they can take in society, and how they are expected to feel or behave. This moment of assignment is consequently of fundamental importance to a person's life. While this categorization is repeated, throughout our lives, whenever we meet a new person, the first time it happens initiates a process by which a person is recognized by others, and comes to recognize himself or herself, as a member of one of two fundamental social categories: male and female. Once other people recognize the baby as belonging to one or other of these categories, this immediately affects how she or he is handled, talked to, enabled and restrained, the expectations for her or his future and about her or his personality (Smith and Lloyd 1978; Burman 1995; Ruble and Martin 1998). Once the baby has been named as male or female, the process begins through which he or she is claimed, and learns to understand himself or herself, as a member of the larger community of boys and girls, men and women.

My argument in this book is that this process of learning to be male or female takes place within loose, overlapping, local communities of masculinity and femininity practice (Paechter 2003a, 2003b, 2006b). In these communities, children and young people experience what it is to be treated as male and female, and learn what the expectations of males and females are in the communities of which they are members. What this means will be much more fully explained in Chapter 3, but for now an outline will suffice.

A community of practice is, put simply, a community engaging in a shared practice. Novices to that community are seen as developing their expertise in these practices through 'legitimate peripheral participation' (Lave and Wenger 1991) in the practice. Legitimate peripheral participation allows a novice to take part in peripheral aspects of the practice of the community, and to be recognized as legitimately so doing, while gradually being inducted into more central, often more complex, practices. In this process, learners develop not just their expertise in the practice, but also their understanding of and embeddedness in the culture that surrounds it, and what it means to take on the identities that go with being a central participant. Through the acknowledged legitimacy of their participation, they learn how to be full participants in the community of practice, with all the many and varied social behaviours and relations that this implies. Everyone is a member of a large number of communities of practice, of masculinity or femininity and of other things, so that a person's identity is developed at least partly in the overlap between these communities (Wenger 1998).

Practice is central to participation in any community of practice: it is what makes the community what it is. Key to the coherence of a community of practice are three dimensions: mutual engagement, that is, being engaged with each other; joint enterprise, or taking part in a collective endeavour; and shared repertoire, having in common actions, behaviour and language that are particular to and shared by the group (Wenger 1998). These act to bring the community together, to give it a sense that it is a community, and to demonstrate the nature of the community to both members and outsiders. Shared local practices of masculinity, for example, both allow members of that community of practice to recognize others, not just as men, but as men like them, and make it possible both for women and for men from different local groups to understand themselves as different.

When a baby is named as a boy or a girl, he or she is thus placed in a constellation of overlapping local communities of practice of masculinity or femininity, through which he or she will learn, from more established group members (such as parents and siblings) what it is to be male or female in that community. Thus boys can be seen (broadly) as apprentice men, learning, through observation of the men they encounter and peripheral participation in their activities, what it means to be a man in the local communities of practice in which they live. Girls, similarly, are apprentice women, taking part with adult women in activities pertaining to womanhood in those communities. At the same time, children are full members of child or adolescent communities of masculinity or femininity practice, which will have their own dominant and subordinate ways of being.

A community of practice is, thus, a location in and through which individuals develop their identities, in relation both to other members of the community and to members of other communities. It is where individuals come to understand what it is to have a part in community identity, and the behaviours and practices that are associated with it. In the case of the constellation of communities of masculinity and femininity practice with which we are concerned in this book, these are where babies, children and young people learn what it is to be male or female, how this means they can think about themselves, and the implications of these for what they can say, do or be.

Before we can consider the nature of communities of practice in detail, however, we need to explore some underlying issues. In the rest of this chapter, I will explain some of the other key concepts that underpin this book. First, I will consider a dualistic distinction between mind and body that stems from Descartes and continues to permeate many of our understandings of ourselves as embodied beings. This leads into a discussion of the language around sex and gender, masculinities and femininities, and I will explain how I use and understand these terms. I will then turn to the related question of how masculinities and femininities are at least partially performed, and the importance of bodies in this. Finally, I will introduce my theoretical position on power relations, which I will develop further in the next chapter.

Mind/body dualism and the legacy of Descartes

Much of Western thinking about the relationship between the mind and the body arises from a dualism originating in the work of Descartes in the early seventeenth century. Descartes was concerned not with the mind and the body as such, but instead with trying to understand what could be known to be true. His approach to this was to reject as false anything about which there might be the smallest possible doubt, and then see what remained. The evidence of his senses had to be rejected, because he knew that 'they sometimes play us false' (Descartes 1968: 53). The person who rejected that evidence, however, could be known to exist, because of his very ability to do this:

> I became aware that, while I decided thus to think that everything was false, it followed necessarily that I who thought must be something; and observing that this truth: *I think, therefore I am*, was so certain and so evident that all the most extravagant suppositions of the sceptics were not capable of shaking it, I judged that I could accept it without scruple as the first principle of the philosophy I was seeking.
> (Descartes 1968: 53–4, emphasis in original)

From this founding proposition, in *Discourse on Method*, Descartes moves in the *Meditations* to a superficially similar, but much more radical, proposition – that the self is located purely in the thinking mind, and not in any way in the body:

> I rightly conclude that my essence consists in this alone, that I am a thinking thing, or a substance whose whole essence or nature consists in thinking ... I, that is to say my mind, by

which I am what I am, is entirely and truly distinct from my body, and may exist without it.

(Descartes 1968: 156)

It is necessary to understand here that Descartes' mind/body distinction is a formal dualism, not simply a difference between two equal aspects (Gatens 1991). In a formal dualism, 'categories are not only constituted hierarchically (for example in gender categories the masculine/male is given superiority), but one of the categories is *constituted within binary logic as nothing*' (McFarlane 1998: 206, emphasis in original). This means that in the Cartesian binary, once the mind is constituted as the seat of identity, the body is completely excluded from consideration; it is simply another part of that which is not the mind. Consequently, Descartes' dualistic split between mind and body constitutes in many ways a repudiation of the body. Identity becomes located entirely in the mind, something that is understood as independent of the body and its form. This clear separation between mind and body was fundamental to Enlightenment thought, and has remained with us in myriad forms. It is this focus on the mind as the key seat of identity that allowed theorists in a number of fields to posit a distinction between sex and gender. Unfortunately, this also meant that the distinction was itself set up dualistically.

Masculinities and femininities

In the second half of the twentieth century, most people writing about sex and gender in the anglophone West – though not always in other language communities (Moi 1999; Rhedding-Jones 2003) – made a clear distinction between 'sex' and 'gender' as terms. Stoller, for example, whose definitions influenced and were followed by many subsequent writers, draws a clear distinction between the two:

The word *sexual* will have connotations of anatomy and physiology. This obviously leaves tremendous areas of behavior, feelings, thoughts, and fantasies that are related to the sexes and yet do not have primarily biological connotations. It is for some of these psychological phenomena that the term *gender* will be used.

(Stoller 1968: viii–ix, emphasis in original)

According to this distinction, biological sex was seen as something relatively fixed, a 'truth' of the body, while gender was more contingent.

Sex was seen as dichotomous, while gender, defined by Stoller (1968: 9–10) as 'the amount of masculinity or femininity found in a person', was, on the one hand, treated as variable and, on the other, formed a parallel social dichotomy, with two genders corresponding to two sexes.

At the time, this distinction was particularly useful for two groups: feminizts and transsexuals. For both it served essential purposes in the particular battles being fought at the time. For feminizts it was an important part of the argument that biology was not destiny, that women's lives did not have to follow their biological functions as childbearers (Braidotti 2002). For transsexuals, it allowed the possibility of their existence, by reinforcing the idea that a fundamental aspect of identity, gender, could be separated from the physical appearance and functioning of the body. It made transsexualizm a coherent possibility. It is therefore understandable that the idea that sex and gender were independent gained such currency during the latter half of the twentieth century.

At the same time, the distinction between sex and gender has had a number of rather less benign effects. First, because of its relationship with the mind/body split, it is essentially dualistic. However, it is an unusual dualism, as either half can be the main term. Depending on one's theoretical or political position, either the mind or the body can be seen as all-important for identity and behaviour. Setting up sex and gender in a dualistic relation treats mind and body, or specifically, the sense of oneself as masculine or feminine, and the understanding that one is physically male or female, as separate and distinct. It also gives a spurious facticity to biological sex; it suggests that, while gender is variable, contingent and socially constructed, sex is somehow more real, more solid, more incontrovertible and provable. Bodies, however, are themselves understood and interpreted from within the wider assumptions of particular societies (Laqueur 1990). For example, we expect bodies to be straightforwardly and dimorphically male or female, despite the existence of various intersex conditions, which demonstrate a range of bodily morphologies and chromosomal configurations (Fausto-Sterling 1989, 1993, 2000a, 2000b; Kessler 1998; Preves 2003). Thus the sex/gender dualism can be said to misrepresent the body, to place too great a reliance on its materiality, without taking into account that this materiality is socially mediated and understood. This is not to deny that the physical nature of the body is important; I shall argue later that it is an inescapable part of identity. It is, rather, to remember that even the physical is not just given, but has to be understood and interpreted through social processes.

Second, the dualistic split between sex and gender suggests that questions of identity and behaviour are unrelated to bodies, that the people we are bear no relation to the bodies we inhabit. Quite apart from the increasing evidence that, for example, emotional and physical states are closely linked (Damasio 1994), and that a person's experiences affect the structures of his or her brain (Sacks 1993), this ignores the fact that we experience the world through our bodies (Birke 1999), and other people experience and understand us through the bodily presentations we put before them. Identity must, therefore, be constructed and experienced at least in part through our embodiment (Braidotti 2002): who we are is inextricably bound up with whether we are short or tall, fat or thin, conventionally good-looking, infirm through age or disability, and so on. Even for those people (such as transsexuals) for whom the body is a serious problem, identity is not constructed independently of, but in opposition to it. The body is not unimportant; on the contrary, in such cases its importance – as the 'wrong' body (Prosser 1998) – is overwhelming.

Third, almost from the beginning there has been a tendency to use the two terms, 'sex' and 'gender', more or less interchangeably, particularly in everyday speech (Kessler and McKenna 1978), as if 'gender' were a more politically correct word for 'sex', rather than having a distinct meaning. This gives us, at best, a doubled dualism, so that we end up with a situation of compulsory correspondence between sex and gender, between a person's (outward) bodily form and understanding of him or herself as male or female (Paechter 2006b), in order to keep the two terms operating in parallel. At worst, it makes the distinction completely meaningless, with 'gender' being used in a way which bears no relation to the social at all. Now that the press has started to refer to the effects of 'gender-bending chemicals', which cause fish to change sex (Briggs 2000), perhaps the distinction between sex and gender, even to the extent that it was ever current outside feminizt circles, has broken down so far as to be more or less useless.

Finally, even if we accept that 'sex' and 'gender' are meaningful and distinct terms, having them in a dualistic relation renders invisible their close interdependence. Specifically, it hides the way that the performance of naming a child as a boy or a girl, of declaring a baby's sex, tells the community in which they live, and later, the individual himself or herself, what gender they should be. Because sex and gender have become compulsorily in correspondence, the naming of a baby's sex is also a naming of their gender, with all the assumptions that go along with this.

As a consequence of these difficulties, although I shall use both 'sex' and 'gender' from time to time in this book, particularly in relation to what I shall argue are 'gendered power/knowledge relations', in the main I will refer to 'masculinities' and 'femininities'. I take 'masculinities' and 'femininities' to mean the ways in which we 'do' boy or girl, man or woman (West and Zimmerman 1987): that is, the ways in which we, through our behaviour and attitudes, actions, thoughts and dispositions, demonstrate, to ourselves and others, how we are male or female. This approach, though still far from ideal, gets over some of the problems of mind/body and sex/gender dualism. Being a man or woman, boy or girl, is clearly something that is embodied (Connell 2002), if only because, for most people, these are related to and arise out of our originally assigned sex. It is also the case, as will be discussed in more detail below, that the ways in which any individual can 'do' man or woman are limited and enabled by the actual body that person has. This is particularly the case for children, to whom contemporary possibilities of body alteration are rarely available.

I need to distinguish two related pairs of concepts here. The first, masculinity and femininity, represents group ideas about what it is to be male and female in a particular society. A community of masculinity or femininity practice will therefore construct a communal ideal typical version of masculinity or femininity, which will represent what men and women are supposed to be like in that community. In relation to this, individuals will construct their own masculinities and femininities, which are the ways in which they personally 'do' boy or girl, man or woman, and which will be much more varied; in particular, it should be noted, these can include both masculine femininities and feminine masculinities (Paechter 2006a; Pascoe 2007). Most people will construct masculinities or femininities according to their named, assigned, sex, with girls and women constructing femininities, boys and men masculinities, which will be related to and constructed from (or in opposition to) elements of the forms of masculinity and femininity dominant in their local communities of masculinity and femininity practice.

Thus, in their multiple communities of femininity practice, women and girls both construct a sort of ideal type (or types, different in different communities) of what it is to be a woman (femininity), and, at the same time, develop their understandings of who they are (their individual and group femininities) in relation to that. Both 'femininity' and 'femininities' are relational concepts, but they are relational in different ways. Femininity, while not monolithic, is much more all-encompassing, allowing both men and women to make generalizations (women are like *this*, not like *that*), while at the same time allowing women to construct their individual femininities more or less in alignment with or in opposition to these ideas. Similarly, masculinity is not simply 'what men do'; it is more of an ideal type which encapsulates what ideal-typical men (who may not exist at all, anywhere) are expected to think and do. What this means in relation to our embodiment, and to how we understand whatever is left of the distinction between sex and gender, is that we need to continue to think of ourselves as male or female, with identities that are made up of, among other things, masculine and feminine aspects. These aspects together constitute the masculinities and femininities that we construct, inhabit and perform, at different times and in different places.

Some of these group conceptions of masculinity and femininity are more dominant than others. Connell (1995: 77) notes that:

> At any given time, one form of masculinity rather than others is culturally exalted. Hegemonic masculinity can be defined as the configuration of gender practice which embodies the currently accepted answer to the problem of the legitimacy of patriarchy, which guarantees (or is taken to guarantee) the dominant position of men and the subordination of women.

These dominant notions of masculinity, and concomitant ideas of emphasized femininity (Connell 1987) are frequently taken up by communities of masculinity and femininity practice as they construct group versions of what it might be to be male or female. Hegemonic masculinity, in particular, is useful to groups of men and boys in this regard, because of its importance in supporting patriarchal structures and what Connell (1995: 79) refers to as the 'patriarchal dividend, the advantage men in general gain from the overall subordination of women'. Consequently, while few individual masculinities are likely to be fully aligned with hegemonic masculinity, group conceptions of masculinity may be much more closely associated with it, in order to gain the concomitant benefits. Emphasized femininity is again more likely to be a group rather than an individual construction, and relates oppositionally, or to be more precise, in a relation of Other, of dualistic negation, to hegemonic masculinity.

When I use the terms 'men', 'women', 'boys' and 'girls', this will reflect how a person has been assigned, or the gender that they claim for themselves. This is not necessarily a person's chromosomal or morpho-logical sex, but reflects what they think they are, in terms of a gender label. These terms are neutral as to what a person is like, so that it is possible to have a masculine woman, or feminine boy. 'Masculine' and 'feminine' will be used as descriptors for clusters of behaviours or attributes, which will be related to dominant social conceptions of masculinity and femininity, but without prejudice as to whether these are taken up by or associated with actual men or women. They will be connected, however, to a number of knowledge-related dualisms which stem from the mind/body, sex/gender distinctions, as will be discussed below.

Masculinities and femininities as performed identities

> The abiding assumption of my earlier gender theory was that gender is complexly produced through identificatory and performative practices, and that gender is not as clear or univocal as we are sometimes led to believe. My effort was to combat forms of essentialism which claimed that gender is a truth that is somehow there, interior to the body, as a core or as an internal essence, something that we cannot deny, something which, natural or not, is treated as given.
>
> (Butler 2004: 212)

Seeing gender as the ways in which we 'do' boy or girl, man or woman, implies that it is not a given, but something that is constantly demonstrated, or performed. A person's masculinity or femininity is not innate, is not natural, but instead is something that is learned, constantly reworked and reconfigured, and enacted to the self and to others. Masculinity and femininity are active states; they are not just what we are, they are what we do, how we appear, how we think of ourselves, at particular times, and in specific places. It is thus a matter, not of an internal essence or core of our being (Mort and Peters 2005), but instead of who or what we identify with, and how we demonstrate that identification to ourselves and others.

Our various masculinities and femininities are constructed as ways of being within particular communities of masculinity and femininity practice, and are likely to change as we move between these communities. Masculinities or femininities, therefore, may be both experienced and performed differently according to the situations in which individuals find themselves; what is understood, experienced and read as masculine in one community may be considered, even from the point of view of the same person, as feminine in another. This again reflects the relationality of these concepts and the ways in which masculinities and femininities are specific and local. Even the relatively crude understandings of 'what men do' held by young children are derived only from their observations of specific men and women, even if they are put into a premature generalization.

In the earlier work on gender, to which Butler refers above, she argued that gender was entirely performative, and consequently tenuous:

> Gender is an identity tenuously constituted in time, instituted in an exterior space through a *stylized repetition of acts*. The effect of gender is produced through the stylization of the body and,

hence, must be understood as the mundane way in which bodily gestures, movements, and styles of various kinds create the illusion of an abiding gendered self. This formulation moves the conception of gender off the ground of a substantial model of identity to one that requires a conception of gender as a constituted *social temporality*.

(Butler 1990: 140-1)

This can be interpreted in a number of ways. I would argue here that it means that masculinities and femininities are not only variable between people, but they are also variable within any individual. Who one can be alters according to where one is, and with whom. It is also the case that the repetition of particular acts (and the non-performance of others) is part of what convinces one of one's own gender and that of others; it is in their practices that communities of masculinity and femininity practice mutually identify and cohere.

That masculinities and femininities are constructed and performed within practice communities also brings to the fore the disciplinary nature of such constructions and performances. In order to remain within a particular community of practice, an individual has to regulate her or his performance so that it remains within the norms of that community. Thus, one does not just get up in the morning and decide to be a particular sort of person; the possibilities for a person's under-standing and performance of self are governed by the communities of which that person is a member and the situations which she or he is in. As Butler (1993: 2) argues, we must not understand peformativity as 'the act by which a subject brings into being what she/he names but, rather, as that reiterative power of discourse to produce the phenomena that it regulates and constrains'.

Although Butler is mainly interested in the ways in which performance is limited by and challenges discourse, I would also argue that the performance of various masculinities and femininities is considerably constrained by the body an individual has. Bodies are not neutral; they are old and young, able and disabled, and these things affect the ways in which we can act and, concomitantly, the people we can be. As Massey (1999: 56) notes, for example, however much we argue that it is society's assumptions and exclusions, rather than bodily form, that make people disabled, 'social constructedness does not deal with the material reality of having your legs ache all the time'. The materiality of the body is inescapable, and affects what can and cannot be performed by a particular individual.

The performance of masculinities and femininities is deeply related to the constant construction and reconstruction of identity. A centrally important aspect of this performance is that it is to oneself as well as to others: it is about saying to oneself that one is this sort of person, and not another sort. We see this particularly clearly when young children posture and act out in front of the mirror; they are trying on identities as adults might try on clothes – and, indeed, as young people and adults do try on and accept or discard particular items of clothing as part of establishing and consolidating the sort of person they are (Hey 1997). The performance of an individual's various masculinities or femininities is thus partly a matter of telling the self to the self. It is about establishing and understanding who one is, about identity.

This performance of the self to the self is particularly important at key points in child development. For young children under the age of 4 or 5 years, the idea that gender remains constant throughout life is not well established. Thus, it is only through the performance of masculinities or femininities that young children are able to understand themselves as male or female; they do not have a sense of this as something that is continuous and unchanging. This means that their performances are likely to be highly stereotyped and much more constrained by local conventions about the nature of masculinity and femininity than is the case for adults or children of other ages. Similarly, in adolescence, there is a process of construction of a potential male or female adult self. While by this stage the range of possible performances is much greater, it remains limited by the constraints of what is considered acceptable within the (often strongly differentiated and boundaried) adolescent communities of masculinity or femininity practice to which young people belong. Furthermore, children are able to be reflective about their performances of masculinity or femininity, and about the implications of these for identity. I have found in my own research with Sheryl Clark, for example, that 10-year-olds can tell you whether they are tomboys or 'girly-girls', explaining these labels in terms of their dress, attitudes and play preferences.

The performance of masculinities and femininities is also, of course, a performance to and for others. Here, even more than to the self, it is successful performance that matters; even transgressive performances only have any point if they are read as such.[1] Consequently, the performance of gender is a reciprocal relation between performer and audience, and its meaning will be interpreted in the relationship between them. As a result, what a performance of masculinity or femininity means, how it is read and understood, will depend on the context in which it takes place and on the practice communities that performer and audience belong to. Both of these may involve differential power relations, so that performer and audience may have a different degree of influence on the meaning, and therefore the acceptability, within that context, of the performance. In order to understand the implications of this, we need now to examine the nature of power, and how it can operate in communities of masculinity and femininity practice.

Gendered power/knowledge, masculinity and femininity

In this book I am taking an approach to power that stems from the work of Foucault (1963, 1972, 1977, 1978, 1979a, 1979b, 1980, 1982, 1988a, 1988b; Patton 1979; Martin 1988). This understanding of power regards it as something that, rather than residing in individuals or institutions, permeates society in a complex, interweaving and capillary manner, through human interactions, institutional relations, and spatial configurations. Power, argues Foucault (1978: 93), is omnipresent,

> because it is produced from one moment to the next, at every point, or rather in every relation from one point to another. Power is everywhere, not because it embraces everything, but because it comes from everywhere ... power is not an institution, and not a structure; neither is it a certain strength we are endowed with; it is the name that one attributes to a complex strategical situation in a particular society.

Power, understood this way, is fundamentally relational; it operates through interactions, which are mobile and constantly changing. Indeed, it has to be mobilized, put into action; without mobilization, power cannot exist (Foucault 1982; Allen 2003).

Because power is woven through the social fabric, it cannot be understood as being imposed from above. Foucault (1980: 99) argues that we must have 'an *ascending* analysis of power' (emphasis in original), starting with small, individual mechanisms and interactions and moving towards the more general. Thus we have a focus that is not so much on who wields power, but the processes through which power relations come to be mobilized in one way rather than in another.

The relational and capillary nature of power means that resistance is relational and capillary also. Foucault (1978: 95–6) argues that wherever there is power, there is resistance; the two go together, inextricably linked:

> Where there is power, there is resistance, and yet, or rather consequently, this resistance is never in a position of exteriority

> in relation to power ... [The existence of power relations]
> depends on a multiplicity of points of resistance: these play the
> role of adversary, target, support, or handle in power relations.
> These points of resistance are present everywhere in the power
> network ... there is a plurality of resistances, each of them a
> special case.

Thus, whenever we think about power, and how it is configured, for
example, within a community of masculinity or feminity practice, we
have also to think about resistance, and to trace its points and pathways.
This is partly because, as Foucault (1982: 221) points out, 'power is
exercised only over free subjects, and only insofar as they are free': slavery
is not a power relationship, but one of constraint. If power is understood
in this way, to include and depend upon human freedom, then it is clear
that it will have, at all times, to include and depend upon resistance.

Power is also, in this view, deeply integrated and implicated within
knowledge; power is understood as producing knowledge (Foucault
1980). Foucault indicates this by using the combined term, power/
knowledge:

> We should admit ... that power produces knowledge; ... that
> power and knowledge directly imply one another; that there is
> no power relation without the correlative constitution of a field
> of knowledge, nor any knowledge that does not presuppose and
> constitute at the same time power relations.
>
> (Foucault 1977: 27)

The mutual implication of power and knowledge is particularly
important in this book for two reasons. First, power/knowledge is always
gendered. This is because knowledge is gendered (in different ways at
different times), and the gendered nature of knowledge has effects at the
level of power (Paechter 2000). Specifically, in terms of the issues we are
considering here, there is a complex relationship between knowing and
claiming one's sex (in the sense of knowing that one is male or female),
performing particular forms of masculinity or femininity (some of which
are more powerfully positioned than others), and an individual's ability
to make good the claim that such performances can be taken to
demonstrate the legitimacy of the underlying claim to that sex. Knowing
one's sex, and having others know it, places a person immediately in a
power/knowledge relationship in which many other things are implied,
in terms of that person's potential to operate in the world in particular
ways. Much of what a child or young person is doing in learning to be a
full participant in a local community of masculinity or femininity

practice, is preparing herself- or himself to make good such claims, in a society in which masculinity is more highly valued, and therefore requires greater proofs than femininity.

This requires some knowledges to be retained for masculinity, and for hegemonic masculinity in particular. Historically, those knowledges which have been seen as powerful at a particular time have been reserved for (middle-class, white) males (Delamont 1994), either through explicit restriction or by being labelled as masculine, which, while not preventing women and girls from having access to them, provides a constraint which can interfere with their claims to legitimate performance of femininity (Paechter 1998; Chapman 2001; Mendick 2006). From the point of view of our interests in this book, this affects the ways in which children and young people construct their masculinities and femininities in relation to schooling; school-based communities of masculinity and femininity practice will incorporate particular power/ knowledge relations which will affect how boys and girls can be, what they can be seen to succeed at, and what they can study.

Panoptic surveillance

An important way in which power/knowledge relations are enacted in social groups and public institutions is through the mechanism of panoptic surveillance. Originating as a concept related to physical sites, such as prisons, hospitals and schools, constructed for the purposes of social control and regulation, it has application within much more loosely regulated social groups, such as communities of masculinity and femininity practice. The panoptic mechanisms of these will be discussed in Chapter 3. Here, I will outline its general nature, focusing on the basic mode of operation and its importance for power/knowledge.

The concept of panoptic surveillance was developed by Foucault (1977) from Jeremy Bentham's design for the Panopticon, a model prison. The idea behind the Panopticon was that, rather than being punitive, prison should be a means of reform. Prisoners would consequently be treated humanely, while at the same time they were observed to see if a dispositional improvement had indeed taken place. The Panopticon was, therefore, a mechanism, a disciplinary apparatus, in which transgressors might learn to be good.

The design of the Panopticon was simple. It consisted of a central guard tower, kept always in darkness, with the prisoners in lighted cells around the perimeter. This allowed the guards to watch the prisoners continually, without being seen themselves. The consciousness that one might be being watched at any time, coupled with the impossibility of knowing if one were actually being watched at any particular moment, was designed to force the prisoner to behave well at all times. The intention was that this would require the prisoner to internalize this good behaviour, so that it became part of his or her normal way of being: it would, indeed, normalize the inmate, turn him or her into a regular member of society. As a result of this, actual surveillance was not needed most of the time; it would be 'permanent in its effects, even if it is discontinuous in its action', so that 'the inmates should be caught up in a power situation of which they are themselves the bearers' (Foucault 1977: 201), in effect policing themselves.

Since Bentham's first design for the Panopticon, such disciplinary apparatuses have been built into schools, factories and hospitals; they are used as a spatial disciplinary for the organization of bodies (Foucault 1977; Markus 1993). The idea of panoptic surveillance is thus directly important for this book because of the ways in which children's masculinities and femininities are constructed within schools, many of which are organized in specifically panoptic ways, allowing teachers and other adults constant surveillance of children. More indirectly, but also even more important, panoptic mechanisms pervade social life, so that there are many situations, including within communities of practice, in which panoptic surveillance, of one group of people by another, takes place. Foucault (1977: 216) suggests that

> One can speak of the formation of a disciplinary society in this movement that stretches from the enclosed disciplines, a sort of social 'quarantine', to an indefinitely generalizable mechanism of 'panopticism'. Not because the disciplinary modality of power has replaced all the others; but because it has infiltrated the others, sometimes undermining them, but serving as an intermediary between them, linking them together, extending them and above all making it possible to bring the effects of power to the most minute and distant elements. It assures an infinitesimal distribution of the power relations.

I would further argue that within communities of practice of masculinity and femininity, particularly in early childhood and adolescence, there is a mutual panopticism in which everyone exerts a disciplinary gaze on everyone else, thus ensuring conformity to the collectively constructed concept of masculinity or femininity.

Panoptic power relations are therefore spread throughout society as part of the capillary mechanisms of power. They are part of gendered power/knowledge relations, for they require the observer to know the observed, and the observed, at the very least, to know of the existence of the observer. They are particularly important within communities of masculinity and femininity practice, where they are essential for the disciplinary mechanisms that retain the focus of particular communities on particular forms of practice. It is to these communities of practice, to how they operate, how identities are constructed and maintained within them, and the importance of gendered power/knowledge relations to their formation and operation, that I turn in the next chapter.

Note

1 This is reflected in one of the key distinctions between transvestite behaviour and drag: transvestites aim to convince as the other sex, even if temporarily, while drag is intended to be read as a crossing of boundaries.

3 Masculinities and femininities as communities of practice[1]

> At the factory, at the pool
> At the match or sat in school
> Riding bikes or making deals
> Sat behind a driving wheel
> In the playground, in the pub
> In the bedroom – there's the rub
> Boys impersonating men
> And I should know – I'm one of them
>
> (Robinson 1994)

Identities in communities of practice

As I outlined in the previous chapter, a community of practice is a community engaging in a shared practice, in this case, the construction and performance of masculinity or femininity. In this chapter, I will explain in more detail what this entails, and the mechanisms through which such constructions and performances take place. This will give us a theoretical underpinning for the detailed exploration of particular communities of children's masculinity and femininity practice, to which the rest of the book is devoted.

Approaching masculinities and femininities as constructed and maintained in local communities of masculinity and femininity practice is useful for a number of reasons. First, it helps us to understand the complex relationship between a theoretical approach to gender as something that is performed, and the actual multiplicity of these performances in their social contexts. Because masculinities and femininities are understood as having different meanings in different times and places, treating them as communities of practice allows us to gain a purchase on specific performances and their significance. Masculinities and femininities are not unitary phenomena: how we enact and experience them changes as we move between groups, between places and spaces, and through time. Furthermore, there is a focus on how the community itself is constantly constructed and reconstructed, as individuals learn to participate and, in time, become full members; this is important for understanding how children learn and construct gendered performances within specific practice settings. The dual focus on how individuals learn to participate in a community of practice (Lave and Wenger 1991), and on the importance of acceptable, socially embedded performance as a major factor in full participation in the community, is central to the usefulness of this approach to the understanding of how children learn and construct masculinities and femininities.

Understanding identity as community membership in this way puts participation, and therefore, practice, at the centre of what it means to be a man or woman, boy or girl. Wenger (1998) argues that practice defines a community through its three dimensions of mutual engagement, joint enterprise and shared repertoire. He suggests that, because participation in some senses constitutes our identity, these three dimensions also become central to identity. I would argue that, in the case of local communities of masculinity and femininity practice, it is shared repertoire that is most important (Butler 1993). Shared repertoire here consists of ways of performing the self, such as styles of walking, talking, dressing and behaving, that are common to group members. To be accepted as 'fully masculine' in a particular social grouping, one must therefore display certain characteristics and behaviours; without this, one is not seen as fully part of the group. Hence, it is not simply a matter of claiming membership of a particular community of masculinity or femininity; one has to be accepted as a legitimate participant by those who are already members. Identity can thus be seen as related to a competent and convincing performance of a particular role. It is defined not just internally by the individual but externally by the group's inclusive or exclusive attitude towards that individual.

Second, considering masculinities and femininities as constructed within communities of masculinity and femininity practice treats identity as the negotiated experience of self, as something that is produced in a social context rather than as a given. Wenger (1998: 149) argues that 'we define who we are by the ways we experience our selves through participation as well as by the ways we and others reify our selves'. This implies that our experience of our identity is deeply bound up with our experience of being in the world, as it is negotiated locally through active and participatory community membership. Identity is thus understood through the practices with which we engage, including those that are involved in the construction and performance of particular masculinities and femininities. These practices and performances, through their repetition (Butler 1990), contribute to our constellated understandings of who we are. Thus, for example, by enacting masculine behaviours focused around competitive sports, boys and young men both form for themselves, and project for others, identities that are at least partly constructed around sporting masculinities (Fitzclarence and Hickey 2001). Similarly, 'racial', 'cultural' and class identities are experienced and enacted in relation to each other and to masculinities and femininities as they are understood in specific local communities (Skeggs 1997; Archer 2003; Archer and Yamashita 2003; Connolly 2004), and mediated by the power/knowledge relations within and between these communities.

Third, this approach also treats masculinities and femininities as fundamentally relational, so that group boundaries, understandings and norms are developed in relation both to those 'inside' the group and to those 'outside', particularly through activity around the periphery. Thorne (1993) refers to such activity as 'borderwork', pointing out that *'although contact sometimes undermines and reduces an active sense of difference, groups may also interact with one another in ways that strengthen their borders'* (Thorne 1993: 65, emphasis in original). Thus, she suggests, boys and girls may play with each other in ways that emphasize the differences between the groups, by splitting into oppositional identity-related groups of 'the boys' and 'the girls'. Thus, they develop their group masculinities and femininities by giving emphasis to real or imagined differences while playing down similarities.

Fourth, connected to this relational aspect of identity is the importance that treating masculinities and femininities as communities of practice gives to the idea of identity as a 'nexus of multimembership' (Wenger 1998: 158). This makes identity dynamic: we are not just men and women, boys and girls, but also members of ethnic, classed, family, work and school communities, with which we construct our varying and variable identities, reflecting the Foucauldian idea that 'the self is the site of multiple practices' (Lloyd 1996: 247). The multiple nature of our participation in communities of practice also means that we can see children as moving between successive age-related communities of masculinity and femininity practice, while gradually becoming less peripheral members of wider, adult-centred gender communities. They do this while simultaneously developing membership of other local communities of practice, such as their school class, their friendship group, their family. These local communities of practice, of which they are members, are related to others in constellation-like groupings (Wenger 1998). Local child groups of masculinity and femininity practice are thus linked through these constellations to similar child groups and to communities of practice of adult masculinity and femininity.

Fifth, this model allows for there to be fluid boundaries across and between different masculinities and femininities. This means that individuals do not have to be committed to one way of being themselves, but can take up or perform several masculinities and femininities, at different places and times. Such fluid multiple membership can involve the body, so that the body is differently presented and used in different circumstances and in relation to different identities. These are not directly dependent on specific embodiments, however, although clearly some masculinities and femininities are more difficult for some bodies to perform than others (Skeggs 1997; Paechter 2003b), and will be limited by this. Nevertheless, the fluidity of boundaries within and between masculinities and femininities both allows us to understand how people can conceive of and experience themselves differently in different situations, and points to the ways in which similar performances can be interpreted differently according to context so that, for example, a young woman committed to playing sports can be understood, and understand herself, as masculine in the context of a multifaculty university but feminine in a specialist physical education college.

This is related to a further feature of this approach to identity: that it is understood as a learning trajectory. Wenger sees identity as a work in progress, constantly negotiated and fundamentally temporal. He argues that 'as trajectories, our identities incorporate the past and the future in the very process of negotiating the present' (Wenger 1998: 55). I would further argue that identities and how they are learned are locational: as we move from one place or institution to another, we have to take on and learn to inhabit different identities. This is particularly obvious, for example, when children start school. Not only do parents talk about this quite overtly ('you're going to be a big school boy now'), but also it can be observed that children's experience of themselves as individuals is strongly affected by starting school (Lloyd and Duveen 1992). This continual reconfiguring of oneself as masculine or feminine is partly a process of learning about oneself and partly one of learning how to perform that masculinity or femininity in specific communities, at particular times and places.

Neither communities of practice nor the identities associated with them are formed in isolation; they may affect local conditions, but these are themselves related to more global considerations. Masculinities and femininities, however local in focus, do not form in a vacuum; they are influenced by, among other things, the mass media, popular culture, other local and wider masculinities and femininities, and the interaction of the members of the community with any and all of these. In particular, local masculinities and femininities will intersect with wider conceptions and practices of masculinity and femininity through the boundary work of those whose membership spans a variety communities, such as different 'racial' or cultural groups, in different ways. Thus, although communities of masculinity and femininity practice are necessarily local, their scope goes beyond this, incorporating features which may be common to a much broader constellation of masculinity and femininity practice communities.

Finally, understanding masculinities and femininities as communities of practice helps us to comprehend why gendered social configurations are so resistant to change. Children learn how to be boys and girls, men and women, from more powerful, often older, members of their local communities of masculinity and femininity practice, who in turn developed their own understandings within similar communities. Because of the continuous nature of these groups, they are likely to be slow to alter; even if some members engage with other ideas about ways of being, if they change their practices significantly they may become increasingly peripheral. Consequently, it is likely that communities of practice that are organized around something as fundamental to identity as masculinity or femininity, will tend to preserve the status quo, maintaining and producing traditional gender divisions and practices. Even where significant change or resistance occurs, this may well take place through the formation of new communities while leaving the old ones intact and relatively unaltered in their practices.

This resistance to change is, of course, bound up with power relations. Those who prevent change tend to be those who are central and; therefore, powerful in a particular community: change and resistance threaten their position. Accordingly, I will now consider gendered power/knowledge and how it operates in communities of masculinity and femininity practice, by considering four key dimensions: legitimate participation; power/knowledge and the body; the regulation of practice; and the maintenance of boundaries between communities. These are all central to the ways in which power/ knowledge is configured in relation to communities of masculinity and femininity practice, and need to be understood before we can consider the communities themselves.

Legitimacy

Being a legitimate participant means having the right to participate in a community of practice, according to one's position in the community and in relation to the practice. That legitimacy is relative to position in this way is important; it takes account both of legitimacy of participation *per se* and of the acts that this legitimacy permits. Thus, for example, in Lave and Wenger's (1991) original conceptualization of legitimate peripheral participation in communities of practice, the apprentices on whom they focused were legitimate participants, but this did not mean that they had the right to participate in all aspects of a particular practice. Their apprentice status meant that they were only permitted to take on specific and, at first, relatively low-level tasks. These gradually became more complex and difficult as their skills developed, and at the same time, they became increasingly, and legitimately, more central members of the practice community. Legitimate membership does not necessarily imply full membership, nor full participation rights, as is clear, for example, when we consider the position of child members of local communities of adult masculinity or femininity. They are allowed to participate up to a point, and to understand themselves as future full members of these communities, but their position is both peripheral and subordinate.

Being able to claim legitimacy for one's participation in a community of masculinity or femininity practice is highly important, because it gives access to symbolic and material goods. This is particularly the case for communities of masculinity practice. In most societies, legitimate participation in communities of masculinity practice confers, often through the 'patriarchal dividend' (Connell 1995), significant benefits, such as higher earnings, higher levels of education, greater access to political power in public life, and personal power in the private realm (Connell 2002). These benefits generally outweigh the disadvantages of belonging to some communities of practice of masculinity, such as being more likely to engage in violent confrontation, stressful competition, and unhealthy practices, such as heavy smoking and drinking (Parker 1996; Connell 2002). Consequently, entry into the constellation of communities of masculinity practice, particularly those which are associated with hegemonic masculinity, is worth defending. This is something that is known and understood both by young boys and by adult men, and underlies the sexually exclusive behaviour of many male groups, who reserve particular forms of knowledge, powerful arenas, and social sites to themselves alone. The boundaries of dominant masculine groups are drawn through the derogatory feminization of subordinates, who are declared to be outside even the constellation of communities of masculinity practice. Consequently, boys will stigmatize their more feminine peers by referring to them as 'girls' or 'sissies' (Thorne 1993). This explicitly challenges the latter's claims to legitimate participation in local masculinity practices.

How an individual is legitimized as a member of a community of masculinity or femininity practice is important for understanding the operation of gendered power relations in Western society. The naming of a baby as a boy or a girl, places him or her in the position of legitimate peripheral participant in local communities of practice of masculinity or femininity. Specifically, it explicitly legitimizes his or her participation in these communities. In response to this naming and positioning, particular forms of behaviour are expected from that child, and are elicited in various ways, including praising or emphasizing some forms of behaviour and ignoring or criticizing others (Stern 1991; Ruble and Martin 1998; Paechter 1999).

In the majority of cases, designation of a baby as male or female takes place through a brief examination of the genitals. When a baby is intersex, however, the procedure is somewhat different. Intersex babies are usually sooner or later designated as male or female, as most societies, with a few notable exceptions (Fausto-Sterling 1993; Paechter 1998), find it hard to countenance the possibility that anyone might be classified outside this binary. However, this can take some time and is likely to require different mechanisms for attributing sex from those that are used in the usual course of events. For example, the baby's chromosomes might be examined, or the configuration of its internal organs considered, before a decision is reached. This decision is, however, only partly concerned with the actualities of biology; much of it relates to the more socially-based issue of whether the parents and surgeons consider the child able to be accepted and to have a role as a legitimate peripheral participant in a community of masculinity or femininity (Kessler 1990, 1998): that is, whether the legitimacy of their participation is likely to come under challenge or scrutiny.

I would like to add a couple of caveats here. First, I am not usually in favour of basing arguments on anomalous cases. While they can be helpful in some circumstances, in others they can lead us seriously astray. Nevertheless, the reactions of parents, doctors and others to the birth of an obviously intersex baby do illuminate the importance given by most, if not all, societies to the categorization of individuals as male or female. Second, I am aware of the ethical issues arising from writing, as a non-intersex person, about those people who are intersex. I would not wish to silence their voices, nor would I wish to use their experiences 'merely to illustrate the social construction of binary sexes' (Koyama 1995–2003). In discussing what happens to intersex babies and their parents, I hope to remain mindful of these issues.

What happens when an intersex baby is named as male or female, sometimes after extensive investigation, is that an 'expert' gives the baby a label which explicitly legitimates that child's participation in the constellation either of masculinity or of femininity practices. It seems to be agreed by these 'experts', by most parents, and by the intersex community (Intersex Society of North America 1995–2003), that this process is very important. This seems to be at least in part a matter of starting the process of developing a shared history with other members of local communities of masculinity and femininity practice, from the moment of birth or, as soon as possible afterwards. This reflects the importance of personal history and continuity as factors in identity (Hacking 1995). Wenger (1998) argues that shared histories are fundamental to learning and identity formation within a community of practice; part of what one gains through participation is this sense of a communal past. The labelling of a child as male or female, as soon after birth as possible, begins this process, placing the child in a particular community of masculinity or femininity practice, treating them according to the ways in which legitimate members of that community are usually treated, and starting off the process of mutual engagement in shared practice, which in turn, will develop into a personal trajectory of relationship with the community and with the practice.

The labelling of an individual as male or female, as early as possible in their life, is thus considered essential to their participation in the relevant community of masculinity and femininity practice. Traditional treatment for intersex babies has also involved surgery that attempts to bring the child's body into as close conformity as possible with the accepted 'norm' for a child of that sex (Money and Ehrhardt 1972; Kessler 1990). It is important to emphasize that such treatment is increasingly being challenged by intersex groups and others, not least because the definitions of 'normal', particularly in the USA, are very narrow, the surgery is invasive, risky, mutilating, may include removal or impairment of orgasmic potential, may not even be as cosmetically convincing as some surgeons claim (Kessler 1990, 1998), and is usually irreversible (Dreger 1995–2005). My interest, however, is in why such invasive and risky surgery is thought, by many doctors working in the field and some parents, to be necessary for these very young babies, who have nothing surgically wrong with them.[2]

Three things seem to be involved here. The first seems to be a sense that part of establishing a shared history within the local community of masculinity or femininity practice is physical conformity to some kind of norm. There seems to be a belief that unless the baby's genital appearance and configuration is closely aligned with these supposed norms, then the legitimacy of their participation in the community will be at risk.[3] Second, and in the context of these genital norms being all-important, is the issue of shared history and continuity of memory. The argument seems to be that if the surgery is carried out sufficiently early in life, the child will not remember that her or his body was once different. This seems to associate identification of oneself as male or female totally with one's genital configuration. Third, community boundaries are being reinforced through a constructed illusion of clear anatomical differences between men and women; the considerable variations in genital appearance and chromosomal configuration are masked through surgery that makes as many people as possible conform to a standard model.

All three of these issues are fundamentally connected with power/knowledge and with the relationship between the outward appearance of the body and the inner understanding of one's gender. It would appear that, from the point of view of medical professionals working with the parents of intersex children, one's sense of belonging to the constellation of communities of practice of masculinity or femininity is, in part at least, dependent on one's body's conformity to a particular, and somewhat arbitrary norm (Kessler 1998). This is a claim that is obviously open to dispute. Although bodies are important aspects of ourselves, it is clear from other contexts that, once established, our sense of our legitimate participation in a constellation of communities of masculinity and femininity practice does not change as our bodies do. Women who have had their breasts or uterus removed, for example, may feel in some ways less feminine, but they do not see themselves as non-female.

Furthermore, the decisions taken about and operations proposed and often carried out on intersex babies are grounded in beliefs about bodies that are fundamentally connected with gendered power/knowledge relations. In particular, the greater salience of the penis than of the vagina in assigning sex to a naked body (Kessler and McKenna 1978) demonstrates the dominance of markers of maleness over those of femaleness. Kessler (1990) reports that the guidelines for gender assignment of intersex infants focus almost exclusively on the viability, or otherwise, of the penis, in terms of its visual appearance and related socially symbolic role rather than its physical function. Put simply, the question is asked, Is this penis long enough to be convincing throughout childhood and into adult life? If it is considered too small, the child is likely to be reassigned as female, the testes removed and a vagina and related outer genitals constructed (and the child given hormones to feminize her body at puberty). This differential clearly reflects gendered power/knowledge relations in wider society:

> The formulation 'good penis equals male; absence of good penis equals female' is treated in the literature and by the physicians interviewed as an objective criterion, operative in all cases. There is a striking lack of attention to the size and shape requirements of the female genitals, other than that the vagina be able to receive a penis.
>
> (Kessler 1990: 20)

Quite apart from the fact that even the viability of the vagina is only considered in terms of its potential for penetration by a male, the gendered power/knowledge relations involved here are clear. This bias in the assignment of sex suggests that only those individuals who can clearly be seen to fit firmly into a set of physical criteria for maleness will be allowed to join communities of practice of masculinity. All others will be treated as females and assigned to the constellation of communities of practice of femininity, which is treated as a sort of dumping ground for those of us who are deemed to be not-male.

That this should be the case is not really surprising. Communities of practice of masculinity remain relatively powerful compared to those of femininity. It is generally the case that powerful communities tend to police their boundaries strongly in order to retain the 'purity' of the community. To allow someone with a 'dubious' claim to masculinity, in a situation in which this is associated with penis size, to be accepted as a legitimate participant is to blur the boundaries of the practice community and lay it open to 'pollution' by outsiders. This means that maleness has to be earned. Femaleness is what is left to those of us who are not, usually because of the visual appearance of our bodies at birth, able to make a legitimate claim to membership of a community of masculinity practice.

Power/knowledge and the body

Legitimacy is thus connected to embodiment in multiple ways. Not only is legitimate peripheral participation in local communities of masculinity and femininity practice in most cases initially conferred on the basis of bodily forms, but we continue to use an individual's appearance to confirm or question their membership of particular communities in both casual and more significant encounters (Kessler and McKenna 1978; Halberstam 1998). In this respect, the body can be said to be a reified marker of membership of the community of practice.

Reification is the process of taking practices and using them to signify community membership. Wenger argues that, alongside participation, reification is fundamental to the negotiation of meaning within communities of practice:

> I will use the concept of reification very generally to refer to the process of giving form to our experience by producing objects that congeal this experience into 'thingness'. In so doing we create points of focus around which the negotiation of meaning becomes organized.
>
> (Wenger 1998: 59)

What this means is that certain concepts become reified as symbolic artefacts and practices; they may then be used as markers of recognition of membership of a particular community. Reification can refer to both a process (by which something becomes reified) and a product (the reified object, practice or process), but to be meaningful it must be incorporated into a local practice. In this way, the products of reification are reflections of the practices of a community.

In the case of communities of practice of masculinity and femininity, bodily form is, as we have seen, a particularly strong marker of potential and actual membership of such a community of practice; the body is a reified object in this respect. However, because the body and, more particularly, the genitals are not always clearly visible, particularly in everyday encounters other, at first sight more trivial, indications can be significant in specific situations. This is because gender dualism is so fundamental to most human societies that we feel uncomfortable if we are unsure if a person we encounter is male or female (West and Zimmerman 1987; Donath 1999; O'Brien 1999). Consequently, other markers of maleness and femaleness may be used, such as, in the case of adults, evidence of secondary sexual characteristics, even if other common markers, such as hairstyle and dress, are ambiguous. With children, however, such characteristics are not available; this is one reason why child communities of masculinity and femininity practice have such strong rules governing what is permissible for boys and girls. Reified objects, such as hairslides and styles or colours of clothing (Bem 1998), become, in such cases, essential to the policing of the borders of these child communities.

The body is also implicated in the reification of particular knowledges as markers of masculinity practice. In relations between communities of practice, masculine-marked knowledges have enormous significance in claiming both material and symbolic goods and in preserving asymmetric power/knowledge relations between men and women. What these knowledges are varies over time (Delamont 1994), but there has been a tendency in the West since the Enlightenment to valorize decontextualized and disembodied knowledges as masculine. This has meant that hegemonic masculinities have been connected particularly closely with such knowledge forms. Disembodied knowledge may, of course, itself be knowledge about the body; indeed, the scientific understanding of the body underpins the development and proliferation of forms of power (Foucault 1978). This knowledge of the body is, however, at a distance; it is of the body as an object of science. Indeed, it could be argued that the development of bio-power, the power 'to take charge of life' (Foucault 1978: 144), parallels the disappearance of the body as overtly significant to powerful subjectivities. Knowledge of others' bodies and the use of this to control them take place in a context of denial of one's own body and the relevance of its experience.

Embodied knowledge, that is knowledge through the body is, on the other hand, associated more closely with subordinate groups, such as women, black people and working-class males (Willis 1977; hooks 1982; Hekman 1995). The most obvious group that has been treated in this way is the constellation of communities of practice to which most women belong, because of the female capacity for pregnancy and childbirth, which was seen by Enlightenment thinkers to tie them permanently to their bodies. Other groups perceived as giving particular importance to the body are also disadvantaged in this way in intergroup power/knowledge relations. Black people, because of their history of being treated simply as bodies when in slavery, are another clear case. Working-class men also suffer from this stigmatization. Although a strong and muscular bodily form is often an important reified marker of full membership of local dominant working-class masculinities (Connell 1995), such dominance has not got working-class men very far in terms of wider power/knowledge relations, including access to secure employment or material goods (Willis 1977; Skelton 2001).

The regulation of practice

Practice is central to identity and to participation within a community of practice. It is practice, in essence, which defines the community: a community of practice is a group of people who do things in a particular way. Shared practices are, thus, what holds the community together, what makes mutual recognition possible, and it is through observation of and participation in shared practices that peripheral members of a community learn to become full members. Lave and Wenger (1991: 95, emphasis in original) argue that legitimate peripheral participation:

> crucially involves *participation* as a way of learning – of both absorbing and being absorbed in – the 'culture of practice' ...
> From a broadly peripheral perspective, apprentices gradually assemble a general idea of what constitutes the practice of the community. This uneven sketch of the enterprise might include who is involved; what they do; what everyday life is like; how masters talk, walk, work and generally conduct their lives; how people who are not part of the community of practice interact with it; what other learners are doing; and what learners need to learn to become full practitioners. It includes an increasing understanding of how, when and about what old-timers

collaborate, collude and collide, and what they enjoy, dislike, respect and admire.

Learning the practice of a community is consequently about learning how to be, and communities of masculinity and femininity practice are no exception to this. Learning full participation in a community of masculinity or femininity practice is about learning one's identity and how to enact it. This is, of course, an embodied identity; one is not just developing an outlook on life, opinions and judgements, or acquiring knowledge that is particular to the group. The learner learns how to move, how to speak (Eckert and McConnell-Ginet 1992), how to behave; in short, how to perform that identity. This embodied performance of community membership is crucial both to legitimacy and to full participation.

This learning takes place in various ways, centred around the learner's participation in the community which they are joining and their emulation, within the community, of central members of that community. This means that, for example, children learn, as they grow up, what are the essential aspects of being a man or a woman in the local communities to which they belong, and they learn to take on these dispositions and behaviours while rejecting or discarding others. The processes through which this happens may be overt (big boys don't cry) or more subtle (ignoring a girl's request for a train set or a boy's for a baby doll), but they construct and reinforce the full members of the community in their position as critical reality definers for that community. It is they, not the peripheral members, who are able to decide what is to 'count' as appropriate behaviour for males and females.

These full members are often adults, but may also be other children: in children's own communities of masculinity and femininity practice some children will be central and others peripheral, and it will be the former who can regulate and enforce what counts as appropriate behaviour within each community. These definitions of what it is to be male and female within a particular community may be established in relation to other communities of practice, either in conformity with them, or oppositionally. In either case, full members of the community are treated as having knowledge about appropriate and inappropriate behaviour within that community, and have the power to enforce that behaviour, for example, by excluding or stigmatizing those peripheral members who do not conform to these definitions.

Lave and Wenger (1991) argue that practice is fluid, that the practices of a particular community are constantly being shifted, negotiated and reinvented. It is the full members of any community, however, who are able to facilitate or prevent these changes, because they are seen as the custodians and enactors of knowledge of what it is to be a full member of a community of practice. Although, as Wenger (1998) suggests, meaning is negotiated within communities of practice, this negotiation can never be power neutral. Different individuals within a group come from different positions and have different possibilities of mobilizing power to their advantage, and a person's value to the community affects what is actually negotiable. Those who are at the centre are thus far more likely to be able to ensure that their meanings prevail. Furthermore, it is these people who have the most to lose from change, and the most to gain from the preservation of the status quo. Redman (1996) points out that dominant groups are heavily invested in those practices and ways of being which preserve this dominance, so that, for example, working with hegemonic masculine groups towards greater equality is, in effect, 'empowering men to disempower themselves', and thus unlikely to be a straightforward task. Consequently, those at the centre of local communities of practice, especially if those communities come together with similar groups to form dominant constellations within a wider society, are able to have much greater control over the meaning of particular identities and what it is like to take these up. Established members, to a large extent, are able to ensure that the local community of masculinity or femininity practice remains more or less as it is, configured in the interests of those full members and supporting their established identities.

Resistance to the established norms of the dominant group within a local community of masculinity or femininity practice, while always possible, comes at a price, which may include permanent peripherality or even expulsion from the group. The taken for granted understandings of full members of the community of practice, can thus function as a repressive discourse that has significant effects on possible forms of identity. In order to take up alternative identities, individuals may be forced to move to an outbound trajectory from a local community of masculinity or femininity practice, joining with others to form alternative, more congenial communities. As Hekman (1995: 82) argues: 'We can accept the script that is written for us, or, alternatively, piece together a different script from other discourses that are extant in our particular circumstances.' How possible this is, however, varies according to the situation. For children at school, for example, it may be hard to find others with whom to establish an alternative community (Renold 2005); the only possibilities may be the extreme one of removal of oneself from the situation (through truancy, home education or change of school) or acceptance of long-term marginal status. The latter can be very painful, particularly for children and adolescents, for whom belonging is very important (Head 1997).

Boundary maintenance

Wenger (1998) argues that practice is a source of coherence for a community: it brings the community together around what the individuals recognize themselves as sharing. Because of this, there have to be boundaries between what is part of group practice and what is not. If these boundaries are too broadly drawn or too fluid, the community will lose coherence, and members will start to feel uncertain about their membership and how it relates to identity. Full members of the community have a key role in drawing and maintaining these boundaries, by putting pressure on peripheral members to conform or leave. Related to this is the power of full members to confer this status on others. If a member of a group continues to operate around the boundaries between the group and the outside, he or she is unlikely ever to be permitted full participant status. This can happen, for example, to gay men or lesbians in some adolescent or adult communities of masculinity or femininity practice, or to non-macho boys or athletic girls in child communities.

The establishment of the boundaries of a community of practice may involve the coercive exclusion of others and a claiming of superiority for members. This is particularly important for communities of masculinity practice, which are defined in part through the Othering of outsiders (Paechter 1998). Such Othering is especially strong among those whose participation in more dominant communities is in some way peripheral or in question, such as children and adolescents. While the symbolic and actual exclusion of the Other is most obvious in extreme forms of hypermasculinity, where the rejection of practices associated with the other gender is fundamental to group identities and cohesion, this also takes place within other specific localized masculinities: for example, middle-class 'new men' define their own forms of masculinity partly through a rejection of the macho (Connell 1995).

While this coercive exclusion of others can be highly problematic for people on the boundaries, it brings significant benefits to those firmly established within the community. The benefits of community member-ship, even when they are not as tangible as those which often accompany masculinity, help us to understand how unequal gender relations are 'reproduced voluntarily through self-normalization to everyday habits of masculinity and femininity' (Bordo 1993: 191). Individuals gain powerful pleasures from participation in communities of practice, even when this is in other ways disempowering. For many, in consequence, the benefits of conformity outweigh those of resistance. Because 'power is exercised only over free subjects' (Foucault 1982: 221), in some senses we choose to participate in the coercive practices of our communities.

The boundaried nature of masculinity and femininity practices within any particular group requires a panoptic process of permanent and continuous regulation of group members. In order both to locate their identities within a particular community of masculinity or femininity practice, and to be recognized by insiders and outsiders as so doing, participants need to ensure that their behaviour is conformable with group norms. Maintaining such boundaries can mean regulating what might seem to be fairly minor aspects of behaviour, especially of physical self-presentation. Teenagers, for example, may police their own and others' expressions of group membership through the clothes they wear and even the places where these are bought (Hey 1997). Distancing oneself from particular clothing styles and sources also distances oneself from other local communities of masculinity or femininity practice; individuals will avoid particular shops or ways of dressing to prevent others making unwarranted assumptions about them.

This constant policing of the self is related to the observation and regulation of one's behaviour by others. The mutual regulation of identity through an internalized observing gaze can be seen as a localized panopticism. First, there is a constant, and therefore internalized scrutiny, which comes from everywhere; as in the panoptic prison, one never knows when one is being watched (Foucault 1977). Here I am following Foucault in regarding the collective gaze as central to the workings of panoptic power relations. Discussing the relationship between the design of the Panopticon and other ideas of the time, he notes that:

> This reign of 'opinion', so often invoked at this time, represents a mode of operation through which power will be exercised by virtue of the mere fact of things being known and people seen in a sort of immediate, collective and anonymous gaze.
>
> (Foucault 1980: 154)

It is precisely through this 'immediate, collective and anonymous gaze' that teenagers expect to be judged as belonging or otherwise. Getting wrong even minor details of self-presentation may result in an individual being classified by others as belonging to a community of masculinity or femininity practice which they themselves reject, and could lead to expulsion from the community with which the person seeks to identify.

This points to the second feature that this mutual observation and relation has in common with Foucault's conception of panoptic power relations: that there are resultant constraints on behaviour. In the Panopticon, the prisoner was forced to adopt certain behaviours in order to appear to have reformed and thus be allowed to leave; it could be argued that prisoners had to demonstrate their potential for membership of a constellation of communities that together constituted 'responsible civil society'. Within communities of masculinity and femininity practice, the continuous mutual gaze similarly requires members, particularly those who are more peripheral, to regulate their expressions of masculinity and femininity so that these conform with group norms. Resistance may have to be quietly or covertly performed.

The situation is complicated in many child and adolescent communities of masculinity and femininity practice because of their close proximity to other groups with whom they are forced to share spaces, such as classrooms and youth clubs. This often results in two or more groups being defined, to some extent, against each other (Eckert 1989). We saw earlier how this can be the case with 'the boys' and 'the girls' (Thorne 1993), but it also happens with regard to different groups of girls and/or boys. When this is the case, behaviours need to be particularly carefully regulated in order to avoid the potential slippage, in the eyes of others, from one group to the next. The mutually observing gaze has the potential to focus, in such contexts, on very small variations and make them highly meaningful to group membership.

It is important to note here that the gaze is both on bodily practices, with ways of dressing, walking, talking and other aspects of self-presentation being crucially important to the initial identification of someone as 'one of us', and on more interior aspects of self, such as beliefs and opinions. The type of music listened to, something particularly crucial for teenage identification, is a further aspect of self which can span both public and private; while teenagers tend to listen to personal music systems ostensibly on an individual basis, the music they contain is often shared either by passing files between machines or through the physical sharing of a pair of headphones (Cullen 2006). These less visible aspects of community belonging, while not so immediately available to the gaze, can, if found to be at variance with group norms, be especially shocking once uncovered. This may be because, particularly in the strongly policed groups of children and adolescents, the mind is the only place where resistance is experienced as possible. Consequently, community members who wish to remain within or retain full participant status of a particular group are likely to monitor the expression of their opinions as carefully as they do their more immediately accessible practices. In this respect, the operation of the mutually observing panoptic gaze in communities of masculinity and femininity practice resembles the operation of 'pastoral power', which 'cannot be exercised without knowing the inside of people's mind, without exploring their souls, without making them reveal their innermost secrets. It implies a knowledge of the conscience and an ability to direct it' (Foucault 1982: 214).

Full members of some communities of masculinity and femininity practice do indeed exercise pastoral power in the sense of protecting more peripheral participants through the examination and regulation of their conduct. Mothers control (or attempt to control) the dress and behaviour of their daughters, in particular, through their injunctions on short skirts, 'too much' make-up, body piercings, and so on (Hey 1997; Skeggs 1997). In doing this they are attempting to preserve their daughters' status as peripheral participants in their own adult communities of femininity practice, while preventing them from being perceived as participants in other communities that are conceived of as inferior or deviant. Pastoral power is here very clearly 'salvation oriented' (Foucault 1982: 214). Daughters may, by conforming to these norms, demonstrate that they have themselves internalized them as part of their legitimate peripheral participation in these adult communities. Others, however, openly resist them, either in order to preserve their peripheral, non-adult, status (Cullen 2005), or as a move towards participation in alternative adult communities of practice with different ideas about what is 'acceptable'.

Third, the penalties for transgression, as in more traditionally panoptic situations, may be heavy. In the Panopticon (as in the modern prison, where, for example, acceptance that one has done wrong may be a condition of early release) failure to conform would lead to longer incarceration. In local communities of masculinity and femininity practice, transgression may result in expulsion from the group (a particularly heavy penalty for many teenagers (Head 1997; Hey 1997)), perpetual peripherality (welcomed by some individuals but highly problematic for others) or even physical attacks, such as 'queer-bashing'.

While this form of panoptic observation is less spatially organized than the more 'classic' forms found in schools, prisons, hospitals and other institutions, it nevertheless has spatial aspects. Any one individual may be a peripheral or full participant in a number of communities of masculinity and/or femininity practice, and these may be spatially segregated. Thus, as a person moves between locations, she or he may also move from overt participation in one community of practice to overt participation in another; different identities (or aspects of identity) may thus be claimed and performed in the different locations.

It is also important to note that, unlike the situation in the panoptic prison, different participants in any one community of practice may gaze and be gazed upon to different degrees and for different purposes. The gaze is not just a gaze of observation and coercion; it is also a gaze of emulation (Woodward 2003). Legitimate peripheral participants in a community of practice are explicitly expected to observe full participants as part of the learning process; it is how they develop their understanding of what it means to be a full participant. The latter, on the other hand, are expected to turn their gaze on those who are peripheral, checking their progress towards full membership (Rapoport *et al.* 1995), while maintaining a disciplinary gaze on other full participants to ensure that the community retains its coherence. The panoptic gaze within communities of masculinity and femininity practice is therefore both symmetrical and asymmetrical, according to the multiplicity of power relations involved; and this differential symmetry is itself continually varying as these power relations change over time and, in some cases, space.

Conclusion

Treating masculinities and femininities as formed within communities of practice is, therefore, a fruitful way of approaching how children learn and construct gendered identities within the home, and in school and peer communities. It allows us to understand masculinities and femininities as particular and local, but connected to wider constellations and social groupings. Treating these communities of practice as key sites for the exercise of gendered power/knowledge relations helps us to understand both how power operates in the formation of masculine and feminine identities and how these are constructed in relation to each other and to other identities and communities.

Understanding how participation in communities of masculinity and femininity practice is connected to the body and embodied performance of self, helps us to see how identity is fundamentally embodied and to challenge the mind/body dualism that has been prevalent in Western thought since the Enlightenment. It also makes it possible to understand how masculinities and femininities, while performative in nature, are not arbitrary; what can be performed is highly dependent on time, place and circumstances, including the power/knowledge relations in a specific context. Furthermore, exploring the salience of the body for legitimizing participation, particularly in communities of masculinity practice, points up both the asymmetries in our understanding of gendered embodiment and the androcentric bias in our labelling of children as male or female.

In the rest of this book I will explore these ideas through the specific contexts in which children construct and learn their masculinities and femininities. This will allow us to see how gender is learned and performed in different situations, how particular gendered power/

knowledge relations become prevalent and then preserved, and how we can act to intervene in this. The latter is important: a major reason for understanding the mechanisms by which particular forms of masculinity and femininity are produced and reproduced is that we should be able to intervene and, even if only in small ways in specific local contexts, to change them. In doing this, as parents, teachers, and others interacting with children, we can start to make the personal political, to act as resistant participants in some of our own local communities of masculinity and femininity practice, working together, with each other and with our children, to form different future possibilities for masculinities and femininities.

Notes

1 This chapter has been developed from three previously published papers (Paechter 2003a, 2003b, 2006b) in which I discuss in more detail how intersex children are named and labelled as members of particular communities of masculinity or femininity practice, and focus also on the learning of adults who wish to change gender. The current chapter concentrates on the issues as they pertain to the learning of children and young people.
2 Some intersex conditions, such as congenital adrenal hyperplasia, can be associated with medical problems which need to be treated for the sake of the baby's health, but these do not involve the genitals and do not require surgery (Kessler 1998).
3 Emi Koyama argues that society's obsession with conformity to ideas of 'normality' means that 'even in the absence of the society's preoccupation with enforcing gender boundaries, intersex bodies [as non-conforming bodies] would continue to be pathologized and treated with invasive and harmful procedures' (*personal communication*, 2003). While I think she is correct in this respect, I do not think it weakens my argument in respect of specifically gendered communities of practice. I am grateful to her for taking the time to engage with me on this issue.

4 Learning masculinities and femininities from parents, carers and siblings

At Cerne Abbas they stood and stared across at the chalky white outline of the Iron-Age giant cut into the green hill. [. . .]

'What's that,' said Lorna. 'That *thing.*'

'It's a giant,' said Frances.

'Like in Jacknabeanstork?'

'Yes.'

'But what's that *thing*. That thing on the giant.'

'That's the giant's thing'

'Is it his stick thing?'

'Yes.'

'My baby budder's got a stick thing.'

'Yes.'

'But I haven't got a stick thing.'

'No.'

'Daddy's got a stick thing.'

'Yes.'

'But *Mummy* hasn't got a stick thing. We're the same, Mummy.'

She beamed and put her warm paw into Frances's.

(Simpson 2001a: 86–7)

Naturalizing difference

Once a baby has been named as male or female, and thus declared a member of a local community of practice of masculinity or femininity, the processes of induction into the norms of that community are set in motion. The baby is at this point an extremely peripheral participant, to the extent that it could be argued that his or her participation is largely passive. Although babies are clearly both energetic and successful in expressing their needs, and those needs can be understood by the people around them as aspects of their masculinity or femininity, it cannot be said, in the first months of life, that a baby is active in constructing the community of masculinity or femininity practice. What does take place, rather, is the construction of the baby's masculinity or femininity by others, through the interpretation and direction of her or his actions.

Cognitive awareness is central to the understanding of oneself within a community of practice. Such understandings, therefore, are not available to very young babies; they develop as they grow and come to comprehend, interpret and construct the world around them. From the moment of their naming as members of a particular community of masculinity or femininity practice, however, babies are taught, in many different ways, how to behave as a member of that community, and have concomitantly different expectations made of them. As they grow older, particularly after the end of their second year, their increasingly mature cognitive processes make it possible for babies to start to develop a sense of the nature of the various local communities of practice, including those of masculinity and femininity, and of their place in them.

In this chapter, therefore, I will examine how masculinities and femininities are constructed for babies and young children by the adult and child communities of masculinity and femininity practice of which they are peripheral members, and how they gradually take over and develop these constructions. To begin with, this construction takes place through differential treatment of boy and girl children, and through parental expectations of and aspirations for boys and girls. As children begin to be able, and are seen to be able, to act consciously for themselves, particular behaviours may be encouraged or discouraged, so that children gradually learn what is acceptable for participants in their local community of masculinity or femininity practice. At the same time, as children start to differentiate between males and females, and to label themselves and others, they begin to develop a cognitive understanding of the differences between the men and women, boys and girls they see around them. At this point, power/knowledge relations within the family become particularly salient, as children construct their understandings of themselves in relation to their interpretations of the gendered power/knowledge configurations of family life.

I argued in Chapter 2 that the dualistic construction of hegemonic masculinity and its negation, emphasized femininity (Connell 1987), supports the domination of men and subordination of women. In order to understand how this works, we need to consider the operation of hegemonic forces generally. The concept of hegemony derives from the work of Gramsci (1971) and is used to explain how it is that dominant social groups preserve their pre-eminence with relatively little resistance from those who are subordinate. In a hegemonic system, the status quo is taken for granted to the extent that it is understood as completely natural and inevitable: the world could not be any other way. Hegemony thus operates at the level of discourse; it structures the ways people can think, so that to think otherwise is to stand outside of society, to think the unthinkable. To challenge hegemonic forces is therefore to stand out against the unseen and unspoken norms of the social world to which one belongs: to ask unaskable questions. That this can be extremely difficult is a measure of the strength of hegemonic power/knowledge relations, which structure the discourses, and hence the understandings, of everyday life.

The key hegemonic force in the operation of gendered power/ knowledge relations is the understanding of difference as 'natural' and therefore inevitable. If differences between men and women, boys and girls, are considered to be innate and inescapable, then so are the power/ knowledge relations that are encapsulated in them. In order for prevalent gendered power/knowledge relations to be preserved, there- fore, a taken for granted assumption of the naturalness of gender difference is essential; it is such assumptions that support hegemonic masculinity and provide men and boys with the benefits of the patriarchal dividend (Connell 1995). Such perceptions regarding differ- ences between males and females, alongside an understanding of the 'natural' as unchangeable through social influence, provide a strong justification for the continuation of unequal relations between men and women, boys and girls, and act as a powerful inhibitor of challenge and change.

It is particularly important to the hegemonic naturalization of difference that it should be perceived from the earliest months, or even days, of a child's life. This allows the division between masculine and feminine to progress seamlessly from a child's naming as male or female, and reduces the risk that the naturalization process should be under- mined by apparent similarities at an early age. Establishing the idea of difference between very young male and female babies also means that children grow up with it. It feels part of them, inevitable, thus enhancing the naturalization process.

This naturalization of difference is circular in its effects. Boys and girls are believed to be different by parents, siblings and carers, and so are treated differently, in myriad ways, from the moment of their naming as members of a particular community of masculinity or femininity practice. Partly as a result of this treatment, they do, eventually, diverge, both physically and in terms of their attitudes and desires. This in turn leads to greater differences, all of which reinforce the impression that they are innate and inevitable. Furthermore, part of what is learned by children within their local communities of masculinity and femininity practice is this discourse of natural difference. That there are two and only two sexes, and that they differ from each other in fundamental, bodily-based ways, has underpinned Western ideas about men and women, in both specialist and non-specialist discourses, since the late seventeenth century (Laqueur 1990).

The hegemonic structure is therefore complete. Difference has not only become completely naturalized and taken for granted in discourse and practice; it is also used to suggest that continued differential treatment of males and females is better for everyone, because it provides what each group believes itself to want. Furthermore, such naturalization emphasizes the cohesion and separation of the categories 'male' and 'female' to an extent that goes far beyond established difference, further supporting the dualistic division between male as subject and female as negated Other.

Establishing and maintaining difference

Biological factors

I have argued earlier in this book that our bodies play an important role in the development and maintenance of masculinities and femininities. Specifically, I suggest, the outward appearance of our bodies, and how we are able to use them, limit who we can be, by limiting the selves we can perform. Before I go on to focus in more depth on the social and cognitive processes that affect how very young children understand themselves and others as masculine and feminine, it is also important to note that there are biological processes in evidence here too. The cognitive, environmental and biological are all implicated in the development of children's masculinities and femininities; none of these can be ruled out (Martin *et al.* 2002). My main focus in this book is on the social and cognitive aspects of how we understand ourselves as men and women, boys and girls, but this is not to say that the biological is of no importance. In particular, biological processes act as a trigger for and a limiter on social and cognitive constructions. They do not dictate who we are, but they act alongside, and may modify social and cognitive forces.

It is important to understand, when discussing biological processes, that they are themselves social constructions (Fausto-Sterling 1987, 1989). What we see, when examining the natural world, and how we label it are products of the understandings of the world that we bring to that process. For example, Laqueur (1990) argues that, up until the late seventeenth century, Western societies had a one-sex model of the human body, in which the male and female sexual and reproductive organs were homologous to the extent that the vagina was basically a penis that had moved upwards inside the body (due to the relative coldness of females; if they became too hot, it was believed, they might indeed move outside and the woman thereby become a man). According to this homology, therefore, the testes are the same as the ovaries, the scrotal sac the uterus, and so on. This is clear from anatomical drawings over a long period, in which the vagina looks remarkably like an interior penis, complete with a glans-like structure at the opening. Anatomical drawings continued to have this form for a considerable time, despite the increasing use of the dissection of corpses as a means of gaining information about the body; anatomists continued to see what they expected to be there. Changes in anatomical drawings only appear as the move from a one-sex to a two-sex model of humans began to take hold during the latter half of the eighteenth century (Laqueur 1990).

Fausto-Sterling (2000b) argues that similar processes have taken place regarding our understanding of the actions of hormones, such as testosterone and oestrogen, both of which are important in the development of primary and secondary sexual characteristics in primates. In particular, oestrogen and progesterone are colloquially known as the 'female' hormones, testosterone as the 'male', despite both males and females producing both, albeit in different quantities. It is also the case that these hormones have effects other than on sexual and reproductive organs. The oestrogens, for example, seem to have a role in stopping growth in adolescence: boys who have been castrated, and therefore produce no testicular oestrogen, fail to stop growing at the usual time and become unusually tall (Leroi 2003). Consequently, it is important, when considering the action of these hormones, to be aware that we see them through a particular set of lenses, which may influence how we interpret their effects.

We must, nevertheless, consider the possible consequences of biological processes with respect to the development of specific masculinities and femininities. In particular, I would like to examine the effects of testosterone on the developing foetus. For all vertebrates, exposure to androgens (including testosterone, produced by the foetus's own testes in males) causes the masculinization of foetal reproductive organs and potentiates subsequent reproductive behaviour. The effects of testosterone in the prenatal period are generally considered to be organizational, having more or less permanent effects on the structure of the brain. As a result, the later effects of testosterone vary from individual to individual, as they are partially dependent on the degree of prenatal masculinization. Furthermore, both male and female testosterone levels can vary (in either direction) as a result of stress (Udry 2000). This suggests that the most important effects of testosterone exposure for the development of masculinities and femininities occur in the prenatal period. What happens at this stage is likely to have a limiting influence on the ways in which specific masculinities and femininities are constructed through social and cognitive processes.

There is some evidence that this is, indeed, the case. Udry (2000) considered a group of adult women from whose mothers blood samples had been taken when they were pregnant, as part of a longitudinal child development study. He found that the more testosterone these women had been exposed to prenatally, the more masculine they were as adults. By including a (rather crude) measure of socialization processes in the study, through asking the adult women if their mothers had encouraged them to behave in a feminine manner when young, Udry found that, for women whose prenatal exposure to testosterone was low, the encouragement towards femininity by their mothers had a strong effect: those whose mothers encouraged femininity were more stereotypically feminine as adults. For those whose exposure to testosterone had been high, however, such encouragement had little effect, and was, indeed, resisted. While we need to be wary of placing too much reliance on retrospective self-reports of this kind, it is clear that prenatal testosterone exposure does have an effect on later behaviour, and that this is likely to be stronger in males, for whom the exposure is much greater due to their own foetal testosterone production. In the discussion that follows it needs to be borne in mind that children's bodies will have effects on the sorts of people they can be, in invisible as well as in visible ways.

In the remainder of this chapter, I will consider young children's development and construction of masculinities and femininities through social and cognitive processes. This seems to take place through a combination of factors. First, children, from when they are born, are treated differently according to sex by the others around them. Such differential treatment, gradually accumulated, will have effects on how children behave, react, and understand themselves, as well as, to some degree, on brain structures (Sacks 1993; Ruble and Martin 1998; Phillips 2005). Second, there seems to be a universal human urge to classify the world and to relate such classifications to oneself (Martin *et al.* 2002). Given the extraordinary salience of gender in human societies, it is unsurprising that children, from an extremely early age, make these classifications and use them to understand their positions in the world.

Differential treatment of boy and girl babies

From the moment that a child is performatively named as a member of a local community of masculinity or femininity practice, she or he is treated accordingly by both adults and children. Such differential treatment is wide-ranging and appears, initially at least, to be independent of the child's individual attributes, desires and behaviours. This has been demonstrated in a number of ways, using both experimental and naturaliztic situations, and these variations, while sometimes quite small, add up to quite different experiences overall. Furthermore, once a child is handled in a particular way, she or he will learn from or develop in accordance with that treatment, amplifying such differentials and making them more likely to be continued by adults and preferred by the child. A clear example of this is the greater encouragement of boys by adults to make large motor movements (Smith and Lloyd 1978; Ruble and Martin 1998): the more they do this, the stronger they become and the more likely they are to enjoy, succeed with, and therefore make such movements, so that eventually they develop actual differences in size and frequency of movement.

Parents and other adults treat boys and girls differently in a number of ways, some of which are quite subtle, others less so. The bedrooms of male and female babies are decorated differently, even before the children are of an age to express preferences. In a study of children aged between 5 and 25 months, it was found that 'girls had more dolls, pink and multicolored clothes, and yellow bedding; whereas boys had more sports equipment, vehicles, and blue bedding and clothing' (Ruble and Martin 1998: 974). Boys and girls are both bought sex-stereotyped toys and offered them when interacting with adults in experimental play situations (Smith and Lloyd 1978; Stern and Karraker 1989; Ruble and Martin 1998).

There is evidence from a number of sources that parents have differential expectations of their male and female babies. Karraker *et al.* (1995) found that parents rated their newborn girls as finer featured, less strong and more delicate than boys, and that stereotyped perceptions persisted after the first week that the babies were at home. Differential expectations of boys and girls have been shown to exist in situations in which there are no objective differences between boys and girls at that age. One experiment which demonstrates this was conducted by Mondschein *et al.* (2000). The researchers set up an adjustable slope and asked mothers to predict whether their 11-month-old babies would attempt and succeed in crawling down slopes of varying steepness. They found that:

> As in previous research ... there were no gender differences in infants' performance. In contrast, mothers' expectations showed gender bias. Mothers of boys expected their infants to be more successful at descending steep slopes than mothers of girls, they expected boys to attempt steeper slopes than girls, and they expected boys to attempt risky slopes and girls to limit their

attempts to safe slopes. On average, mothers produced estimates 5° steeper for boys' crawling ability than for girls' ability, and 13° steeper for boys' crawling attempts than for girls' crawling attempts. A difference of 13° represents more than 33% of the range in infants' attempts.

We assessed the accuracy of mothers' estimates by computing the difference between their estimates and infants' performance. The average size of mothers' errors has functional significance. Previous studies with these procedures showed that the probability of crawling successfully down slopes drops precipitously from 100% success to 0% success within a span of about 8°. ... This means that, on average, mothers expect their girls to fail when the probability of success is 100%, and expect their boys to succeed when the probability of success is 0%.

(Mondschein *et al.* 2000: 312–3)

Given these differences in expectation, it is hardly surprising that such differences in motor skills and physical adventurousness, while not apparent at 11 months, do develop in the preschool years (Mondschein *et al.* 2000). If parents expect girls to be both fearful and unsuccessful when confronted with physical challenges, they are more likely to protect them from these, preventing them from having the experiences that might lead to later courage and success.

Parents seem to communicate differently with boy and girl children in a number of ways. Stern and Karraker (1989) report that boys are touched more frequently and handled more roughly than girls before 3 months of age, while girls are touched more frequently after 6 months. Wille (1995) notes that fathers are less likely to hold sons than daughters. Boys experience more rough-and-tumble play than girls (Gelman *et al.* 2004), and are more likely than girls to be given whole-body stimulation by adults (Ruble and Martin 1998). Parents have also been found to talk about emotions differently to their young sons and daughters. Both mothers and fathers use more, and more varied, emotion words in conversation with girls, and make more reference to sadness and disliking of events with daughters than with sons. Presumably as a result of this, by 70 months, girls are using overwhelmingly more emotion words than boys; it appears that their emotional socialization has, in this way, been more thoroughly developed.

Some of the ways in which parents communicate gender differences to children may be very indirect (Ruble and Martin 1998). Gelman *et al.* (2004) note that although parents are an obvious source of input into young children's gender constructions, there is little relation between parents' and children's attitudes to gender, with children having much more essentialist approaches which treat boys and girls as opposites. Their research suggests that while mothers' explicit talk about masculinity and femininity may convey a neutral message, there is also much implicit gender talk between mothers and children, mostly initiated by the mother, and sometimes giving messages that conflict with the explicit talk. This occurred especially when mothers and children were looking together at counter-stereotypical images. Mothers tended to embrace the counter-stereotype but at the same time draw attention to its counter-stereotypical nature and thus to the salience of constructions of masculinity and femininity in this context, making comments such as 'I notice something really different about this firefighter' (Gelman *et al.* 2004: 95). In addition, mothers rarely negated children's stereotypes, thus indirectly supporting their essentialist beliefs. The authors suggest that, as a result, children as young as 2 years, while not having an explicit understanding of gender, do demonstrate an implicit understanding, as demonstrated by their tendency to mislabel counter-stereotypical images. Explicit communication of ideas about differences between males and females, predictably, has stronger effects. Children who are encouraged to play in gender-stereotyped ways learn labels for men and women at a relatively early age, and have stronger gender-typed toy preferences (Ruble and Martin 1998).

Older children, particularly siblings, may communicate powerful messages to babies about differences between males and females. Stern and Karraker (1989), in a review of studies of the effects of gender labelling (which consider the extent to which the random label 'boy' or 'girl' given to a clothed baby affects people's responses to that baby), found that there were significantly more effects obtained from children aged 2–6 years than from adults. The children believed that babies labelled as boys were bigger, stronger, louder, faster, meaner and harder than those labelled as girls. Given young children's enormous interest in gender, and their generally stereotyped view of the world, this is not surprising, but it does point up the potential importance of older siblings in developing young children's understanding of social categories and how these apply to them. In particular, it has been found that older same-sex siblings support their own constructions of masculinity and femininity by modelling and reinforcing gender-stereotypical behaviour and discouraging cross-gender play in their younger brothers and sisters (Ruble and Martin 1998).

Cognitive issues: Aligning the self with the local community of masculinity or femininity practice

Humans seem to have a universal urge to order and classify the world: in particular, deciding what are the categorical differences between ourselves and others is an essential component of developing an individual identity. Gender is a particularly salient attribute around which to develop such categorizations. First, as has been explained above, ideas about males and females permeate adult conversation with children from a very young age. Simply through the structure of language, children are offered gender labels for people and, in some language communities, things, long before they can produce them themselves. Second, maleness and femaleness are categories that are related to physical appearance, and children learn very early on not only to distinguish between different individuals, but to group those individuals according to various attributes, including gender, age and degree of familiarity. Third, these categories are constantly reiterated, so that as the child develops her or his own categorical understanding, such ideas are reinforced, undermined and fleshed out through their relationships with the categories of significant others; they are constructed in relation to local collective categorizations.

There is evidence that, with regard to differentiation between males and females, this categorization process begins at a very early age. By the age of 6 months, for example, babies can tell the difference between men's and women's voices, and boys of this age are also able to use hairstyles to discriminate between male and female faces. By 9 months, children of both sexes have the ability to correlate faces of men and women with objects associated with males and females in their own homes. At 18 months, some of the metaphorical associations that go alongside and underpin wider dualistic gender categorizations have also developed, with children of this age linking fir trees, bears and the colour blue with males (Martin *et al.* 2002).

It is also at about 18 months that toddlers begin to be able to distinguish between images of themselves and images of other children of the same age and sex. This suggests that it is around this time that they start to construct their own identities, including their identities as masculine or feminine (Martin *et al.* 2002). By 2-2 ½ , children are able to label themselves as male or female. Ruble and Martin (1998: 991) argue that:

> Because gender is likely to be one of the earliest learned and most salient social categories available, children's identification of themselves as a member of the group of males or females

seems likely to have a pronounced impact on their self-concepts, preferences, and behaviors.

They also note that categorization of people or objects into groups in itself has a tendency to lead to the exaggeration of differences between those inside and those outside of the group. Consequently, young children's emerging identities as masculine or feminine, are likely to be constructed, at least partially, along the dualistic lines of me/not-me, like-me/not-like-me, with children making clear distinctions between their own and the other sex. There is evidence that such distinctions are drawn particularly strongly by boys, as they gradually become aware of the benefits of masculinity (Ruble and Martin 1998).

A key concept for understanding the development of young children's constructions of masculinities and femininities is that of gender constancy. This takes place in three stages. The first, gender identity, is the understanding that one is a boy or a girl, usually achieved at 2–3 years. The second, gender stability, is the recognition that this identity does not change over time, so that girls will grow up to be women and boys men: this takes place between ages 4 and 5 (Smith *et al.* 1998). Finally, children acquire the idea that gender is constant, that is, that someone's categorization as male or female does not change according to activity or appearance. This is usually achieved at between 5 and 7 years of age (Martin *et al.* 2002). Until this last stage has been reached, however, children's understanding of their own masculinity or femininity is precarious. Because self-consistency is a strong need in humans, children who have an appreciation of their own gender but who are uncertain about either its stability or its constancy, are likely to draw much greater distinctions between males and females, in their attempts to preserve their sense of membership of the local community of masculinity or femininity practice (Warin 2000; Martin *et al.* 2002).

Gelman *et al.* (2004) point out that young children essentialize and naturalize gender from an early age, making very clear distinctions between boys and girls, treating them as opposites, and often generalizing from one or two instances to males and females as a whole, so that a child told that a boy likes a sofa and a girl likes a table will assume that another girl will also like the table. Martin *et al.* found it difficult to undertake research on children using gender-neutral toys, as 'children appear to seize on any element that resembles a gender norm in order to categorize it as male or female' (Martin *et al.* 2002: 925). Not only do children exaggerate any differences they see between males and females, however minor, they also misremember gender anomalies as being in line with stereotypes, so that a picture of a girl sawing wood will be remembered as being of a boy sawing wood. (Martin *et al.* 2002).

According to Gelman *et al.* (2004), such distinctions go beyond simple categorization; preschool children treat children behaving in counter-stereotypical ways not just as unusual, but as morally problematic or distressing, and take pains to prevent them continuing (Woodward 2003). Although many of these findings are likely to be related to children's attempts to understand and feel fully part of local communities of masculinity or femininity practice, Martin *et al.* also suggest that children's overgeneralization errors in thinking about gender around age 3 echo those taking place about a year earlier in the development of language (for example, use of 'ed' as an ending for all English verbs in the past tense), suggesting that children may have a more general tendency to use 'active inferential processes based on minimal information' (Martin *et al.* 2002: 925) in their construction of the world.

What is clearly the case is that once young children recognize themselves and others as belonging to the category 'boy' or 'girl' they use their developing understanding of categorization to extrapolate from this distinction to a range of others. In doing this they are both constructing for themselves what it means to be a member of the local community of masculinity or femininity practice, and establishing their identities as legitimate members of these communities. Young children, whose understanding of gender stability and constancy is weak, will therefore tend to hold more stereotyped views than do those in middle childhood, regarding what counts as appropriate behaviour for males and females. Where they get the information required to do this varies, of course, with age and with a child's personal situation. It is likely, however, that for very young children, gendered power relations in family life are significant for their understanding of what it means to be a man or woman, boy or girl. It is to these that we now turn.

Participating in local communities of masculinity and femininity practice: gender and power in family life

It is clear, then, that children, from a very young age, are able to observe and organize information about what it is to be male or female, derived from the world around them. As they grow older, they use this to construct their understanding of themselves, learning from the central members of that very local community, their immediate family, how men and women, boys and girls behave and relate to one another. It is important, therefore, to consider what family life is like, and in particular, how gendered power/knowledge relations operate within it.

Most heterosexual relationships in richer countries are not equal ones, although there is some evidence (Dunne 1997) that lesbian couples may be able to negotiate a greater degree of equality. It is also the case, clearly, that children in single-parent families will experience gendered power/knowledge relations somewhat differently, though as most such families are headed by women, the experience of the mother being the main caregiver, with the father, if he is around, taking considerably less responsibility, will remain a predominant experience for most families. In this discussion, I will focus on the gendered power/knowledge relations between heterosexual couples. It is in families headed by such a couple that many children first develop their concepts of masculinity and femininity.

When a couple has children, there is a tendency for mothers to move to part-time employment, or to give up paid work altogether, where this is financially possible, and therefore to spend considerably more time on childcare than fathers (Valentine 1997; Hawkins *et al*. 1998; Xiao 2000; Nordenmark and Nyman 2003), although the extent to which this occurs varies between countries (Gordon *et al*. 2005). This leads to a number of differences in the approaches of male and female parents to their children. Valentine (1997) argues, with regard to older children, that mothers are more likely, because they see more of their children, to modify previously agreed rules according to circumstances, whereas fathers are more detached and therefore more likely to enforce boundaries in a more uniform way. This also relates to fathers' more authoritarian approaches to childrearing, as compared with mothers' tendency to use verbal reasoning to get children to do what is required. Valentine also points out that, while fathers are spending more time with children than they used to, this is not time alone with them, and is often combined with other tasks: for example, they might drop the children off at school on their way to work. Fathers also tend more than mothers, she suggests, to have their main focus on the children when taking part in activities that are also pleasurable for them, such as watching television or playing football. It is mothers whose weekday schedules have to be reorganized for children, and who mainly deal with doctors and with schools.

Across class and ethnic boundaries, and across the globe, women have the main responsibility for households and children. This is the case whether they work outside the home or not, and impacts differently on mothers from different class fractions: in particular, middle-class women are likely to be able either to 'contract out' some of the work (such as cleaning or childcare) to other people (usually other women) or to work part-time, thus reducing the pressure somewhat (Dryden 1999).

Morley (2000) argues that it is part of the dominant construction of femininity that women are responsible for the maintenance of cleanliness and the management of dirt; historically women have been considered to have the physical and moral health of their families as a prime concern (Paechter 2000). This sense of responsibility for the state of the home and their children is still experienced by a significant proportion of women (Hawkins *et al.* 1998). This can make it difficult for women to challenge a situation in which they do more domestic work (or work overall) than their partners, and several authors argue that instead they use various means to construct the situation as 'fair'. Hawkins *et al.* (1998) note that wives in dual-earner couples do two to three times as much housework and childcare as their husbands, but fewer than a third of them think this is unfair. They found that women were more likely to perceive the division of labour in their households as fair if they felt that it was the result of a mutual decision-making process and they were appreciated by their husbands.

Dryden (1999) suggests that the inequality of household relations is a significant undercurrent to family life, but that both husbands and wives develop a number of strategies to deal with it in such a way as not to upset their sense of love and partnership. In her qualitative study of partnership relationships among 17 heterosexual couples in the UK, she found that both men and women attempted to construct themselves as having an equal relationship, but in different ways. The women often found it difficult that they did more in the house than their husbands, or that their husbands expected particular standards and complained when these expectations were not met. They dealt with this by blaming themselves, either for being 'unreasonable' in disagreements over housework, or for being 'too sensitive' when they were upset by their husbands' complaints. Men tended to share this view of their wives' culpability, drawing on wider women-blaming practices to impact on the specific situation of marital partnership. According to Dryden (1999: 61): 'In fact, interviews provided strong evidence that, where women were challenging, questioning and wanting to make changes to the existing status quo of a relationship, men were metaphorically ' "digging their heels in" and resisting change.' Men also often constructed their wives as 'naturally' better at childcare, making it easier for them to hand most of it over to them, as indeed, many did, not just during the working week, but at weekends.

Nordenmark and Nyman (2003) note that in Sweden there is an official ideology of every individual having a right to economic independence through paid work, coupled with an emphasis on shared responsibility for home and children, but that both paid employment and housework are in practice divided between couples according to traditional patterns. Traditional ideas about family life, they argue, coexist in Swedish families with discourses of equality, which means that inequalities around housework and childcare have to be accounted for.

They suggest that the ways in which tasks are allocated give an illusion of fairness. Housework is thus defined as small daily tasks, and done by women, whereas men tend to do bigger and more infrequent jobs, such as chopping wood and household repairs, which are also more visible as 'work'. Again, couples developed a variety of discourses (such as not including childcare in housework, or downplaying its effect on the individual) which either allowed them to understand divisions of labour as 'fair', or helped them to deal with the issue of unfairness within the overall context of family relationships.

Outside of industrialized countries, there may again be official ideological support for gender equality, but this similarly does not translate into equality within family relationships. Holloway (1994: 249), for example, reports that in Tanzania:

> Traditionally, authority rests with the older men of the community and the man, as husband and father, has head-of-household rights which have not been challenged by a wave of women's liberation as in the West. While women have virtually sole responsibility for childcare, men's legal rights to their children remain almost unchallenged.

Such traditional attitudes meant that even a woman in a senior position could feel that she had to organize the household carefully in advance so that her husband would not be inconvenienced if she had to travel for work. It was also the case that, despite an official policy of equal access to training in the Tanzanian civil service, the usual practice was to ask permission from her husband before allowing a woman to participate.

It is clear from this that power/knowledge relations permeate family decisions and structures. Nordenmark and Nyman (2003) argue that access to leisure time is a significant aspect of couples' understanding of fairness within their relationship, but that different people interpret it in different ways: one of the men in their study, for example, considered all the time his wife spent outside paid work as her leisure time, although she used it mainly for housework and childcare. Dryden (1999) notes, similarly, that there was a tendency for the men in her study to consider themselves free once they came home from work, while the women continued working in the home; men also found it easier to go out alone in the evenings than did women.

Morley (1992), reporting on a study of family patterns of television viewing, notes that, while men tended to watch television with full concentration, women were usually doing something else, such as sewing or ironing. He argues that:

this issue raises the further problem of how difficult it is for most women to construct any leisure-time space for themselves within the home – any space, that is, in which they can feel free of the ongoing demands of family life.

(Morley 1992: 141)

This lack of leisure space is echoed in the lack of private physical space for women in the home (Morley 2000), in contrast to the private study space enjoyed by many professional men (Massey 1995).

While in many families fathers have a lot of overt decision-making power due to their higher earnings, making their wives feel constrained about challenging them (Dryden 1999), power relations within the family may also be instantiated in what at first sight are very small ways. Morley (1992: 147) notes that, in families where a considerable amount of family leisure time is spent watching television together, the father is 'the ultimate determinant on occasions of conflict over viewing choices', keeping hold of the remote control and, in some cases, frequently flicking over to other channels in the middle of programmes. The fathers in his study also had a tendency to impose silence on the rest of the family while watching, claiming their desire to concentrate on the programme as justification.

Walkerdine *et al.* (2001) note the lack of power of middle-class mothers in relation to their young children, whether boys or girls. They argue that the discourse of the 'sensitive' mother, facilitating and supporting the development of her child, positions the mother herself as subordinate even with respect to her child:

The mothers in our study turned routine activities, such as cleaning the fish tank or preparing the muesli, into the basis of an invisible pedagogy, one which taught their daughters to argue for their own power through the use of reason (even to the detriment of their mothers, who could sometimes be rather oppressed by these 'suburban terrorists').

(Walkderdine *et al.* 2001: 173)

What young children see in their homes, therefore, is a pattern in which women are subordinate either to men or to young children or to both, while men are dominant, more directive, and have more freedom both from family responsibility and to pursue their own agendas.

It is clear from a number of studies that these patterns of behaviour are observed by children from a very early age. Martin *et al.* (2002) report that children as young as 2 appear to be able to differentiate between activities usually carried out by males and those by females in their own homes, and to evince surprise when this pattern is not followed in experimental situations. These associations extend to objects in the home. They are fairly strongly entrenched within many households, and appear to follow a pattern similar to that of the distribution of household tasks. Morley (1992) suggests, for example, that equipment used for daily activities with a rapidly consumed outcome, such as the cooker, washing machine or iron, are associated with femininity, those for single jobs with an obvious and permanent outcome, such as electric drills and saws, with masculinity. Given young children's propensity for categorization, such differences will be seized upon and incorporated into their understandings of themselves and how they should behave appropriately as males or females.

Conclusion

Very young children seem to be internally driven to categorization in a situation in which to label according to gender is remarkably easy. Given the salience of gender in contemporary society, and the clarity of gender divisions in many families, it is hardly surprising that this is a major aspect of early categorizations. These emerge as children are simultaneously starting to understand the difference between themselves and others, and to develop their construction of themselves as individuals. It is therefore hardly surprising that many of the ways in which children see the world, and align themselves with it, concern understandings of masculinity and femininity.

The family is an unusual community of practice in this regard, as the power/knowledge relations in it are simultaneously highly apparent and cloaked in discourses of child development, family togetherness and the loving bond between couples. While in many ways power differentials between adults and children are clear and strong, in others they are far more blurred, because discourses around the developing child subordinate the mother to the child's emotional and developmental needs (Burman 1994). Similarly, many aspects of power/knowledge relations between mothers and fathers are hidden from the main protagonists behind the discourses of caring and equality necessary to maintain the peace of family life. This often takes place through a woman's emotional work, which operates to maintain the peace of the family home, in some cases to the detriment of her own well-being.

As legitimate peripheral participants in this very local community of practice, young children observe the actualities of family life (who does what, when, and with whom) and draw their own conclusions about what it is to be male or female in this context. These ideas underpin and are the foundations for their constructed selves, and are built upon as they move into the wider world, particularly when they enter peer communities of masculinity and femininity within group childcare and education settings. It is to these that we turn in the next chapter.

Interventions

Intervening in gendered power/knowledge relations within the family is extremely difficult, partly because they are so deeply embedded in multiple discourses that they are hard to identify, let alone challenge. Many of the messages given to parents by children are contradictory, so that a parent may have a spoken ideology of equality while giving subtle messages about inequality through their own actions or by actively drawing attention to, rather than treating as usual, counter-stereotypical examples. In some ways the most effective thing for a parent to do is to work on the inequalities in her or his own family life and hope that these serve as strong models for the children. There are a few other ways in which parents and carers can intervene, however:

- Provide a wide variety of play materials, toys, dressing-up clothes, and activities. Try to avoid labelling any as being 'for boys' or 'for girls'. Actively encourage counter-stereotypical play. Active and adventurous play in girls should especially be encouraged, given its health benefits in later life.
- Try and be aware of how you approach and handle male and female babies, and actively try to refrain from treating boys and girls differently. This can be quite difficult: it sometimes helps to imagine that the baby is of the other sex and see if that alters how you feel about them.
- Have a variety of examples of adults and children engaged in counter-stereotypical activities in books, pictures and everyday conversation, but, rather than commenting on them, treat them as ordinary, without drawing attention to the salience of gender in this regard.
- Model counter-stereotypical activities yourself, but again without drawing attention to the counter-stereotypical nature of that activity. Children will still make generalizations which ignore your own activities, but they can be challenged.
- Challenge children's generic statements about males and females, so that if a child says, 'boys don't do that', find an example of a boy who does.

5   Masculinities and femininities in early years classrooms

When we slowed to a walk at the edge of the school yard, Jem was careful to explain that during school hours I was not to bother him, I was not to approach him with requests to enact a chapter of *Tarzan and the Ant Men*, to embarrass him with references to his private life, or tag along behind him at recess and noon. I was to stick with the first grade and he would stick with the fifth. In short, I was to leave him alone.

'You mean we can't play any more?' I asked.

'We'll do like we always do at home,' he said, 'but you'll see – school's different.'

It certainly was.

(Lee 2000: 17)

Introduction

The move to nursery or to school is a crucial one for young children. For most of them it is the first time they have had to establish themselves as members of a community of practice without the mediating and legitimating presence of their parents or other important adults. This is a complex process which involves presenting oneself to others, and being recognized, as having a right to membership, as being legitimately one of the group. Consequently, children arriving in an early years classroom have to be much more aware of the rules of membership of the group than has been necessary in the past (Jackson and Warin 2000); there will no longer be the shepherding guidance of these trusted full members, and children will have to work out for themselves what is permitted and what is not. At the same time, they are faced with new routines, which may be more or less consonant with those at home (Connolly 2004), and new ways of thinking about themselves, some of which are emphasized explicitly by parents and others in phrases such as 'you're a big school girl now'. This all takes place during the period, between ages 3 and 7, in which children are developing their understanding of gender as fixed (Jackson and Warin 2000). Consequently, membership of local communities of masculinity and femininity practice becomes extremely salient during this period.

Of course, the age at which children start to attend kindergarten, nursery or school, varies between countries. Many will have some previous experience of group daycare, so this transition may be relatively slow and drawn out (Jackson and Warin 2000). Nevertheless, it represents a period in a child's life during which, for the first time, peers become at least as important for shaping identity and behaviour as are parents (Harris 1998), and dissonances and differences between home- and school-based communities of masculinity and femininity practice may throw both into sharp relief. It is a time when a child may first realise that behaviour and play preferences that are considered quite ordinary at home are subject to censure among peers; that not everyone thinks the same way as they do about what it is to be a boy or a girl; and that conformity to and acceptance within the school community may require the suppressing of aspects of the self that are considered unproblematic elsewhere.

In this chapter I will examine what happens to children at this key transition point from home to school, considering how they establish their legitimacy within the new local communities of masculinity and femininity practice, and how this membership is maintained over time. I will focus mainly on preschool nurseries and the very earliest years of schooling, discussing children between the ages of 3 and 6, in their first encounters with the education system. At this stage, the pedagogic emphasis is largely on learning through play and developing the ability to socialize with peers, though as children approach the end of this age range they may also be expected (more or less so in different countries) to learn conformity to more formal modes of schooling. Thus my discussion will largely concern what happens when twenty or thirty children are brought together for several hours at a time in a semi-formal play-based setting supervised by trained, and often interventionist, adults, although I will also consider, to a lesser extent, the effects of the gradual moves towards the more formal routines of main school life.

It is important to be aware throughout this discussion that schools are sites of normalization: that is, they are places in which the idea of the 'normal' child is constructed. Part of this construction is an understanding that boys and girls behave, think and learn in particular ways, and this affects how they are treated and, in turn, how they behave in the classroom. Furthermore, this process by which children are measured against, and encouraged to conform to, norms of masculinity and femininity, involves, particularly in the early years when education is underpinned by notions of child development, considerable surveillance, as well as the disciplining of children's minds and bodies in conformity with the practices of school life. Thus, as we shall see, children's bodies are regulated and controlled, often in ways that are gendered, so that they may have to wear particular forms of clothing, sit in specific ways, at particular times and in designated places and, at times, to act more as a collective than as an individual body.

As newcomers to the social setting of the early years classroom, children have to establish both their legitimacy as participants in the local child communities of practice, and their position in the power/ knowledge nexus in these communities. Establishing the legitimacy of one's participation in the local community of masculinity or femininity practice is crucial: without this one cannot operate in the strongly gendered world of 3–6-year-olds. Because of the particular salience of masculinity for power relations, such legitimacy is especially important for boys. Browne (2004) notes, for example, that while both boys and girls were clear that they did not want to be the other sex, girls were far less perturbed by the question itself than were boys.

A key issue for a newcomer into such a peer community is thus to establish that one is a 'proper' boy or girl (Davies 1989), in a situation in which one is unclear what this might mean in the new community. Children thus have to use peers and staff for guidance (Jordan 1995), looking both for explicitly expressed rules, such as 'Boys are not *allowed* to play with Barbies' (Blaise 2005: 120, emphasis in original) and for more implicit cues, such as what same-sex peers are doing, or whether one is supported, ignored or mocked if one engages in certain activities. Such processes are typical of what happens when newcomers enter any community of practice in which behaviour is strongly policed or ritualized (Lave and Wenger 1991; Mason-Schrock 1996). In the early years classroom they are crucial: because gender constancy is relatively weak in children of this age, everyone's masculinity or femininity is compromised when a performance transgresses accepted and expected norms.

Woodward (2003: 135) observed that children in their first weeks at nursery were 'dynamically hunting for codes concerning the manner in which females and males are supposed to act'. In the British nursery he studied these were often explicit injunctions from established children to newcomers about what they were allowed, or not allowed, to do. Davies (1989) argues that young children are used to having their behavioural errors pointed out to them by others, and expect this with respect to their performances of masculinity or femininity as much as with anything else. This is exemplified in Woodward's study, in which children were seen constantly to reinforce nursery rules with each other, by issuing reminders or reprimands to transgressors:

The newcomers soon came to be adept at interpreting the import of a diversity of often complex and 'Byzantine' nursery involvements. They assessed their new companions' reactions and the information they provided as to the socially 'correct' forms of male and female behaviour. 'Only girls hold hands, Barry ...!' snarled Duncan ... 'I'm not a girl!' pleaded Barry.

(Woodward 2003: 164–5)

Establishing legitimacy in this way can require a child to make explicit and immediate compromises in conformity to local constraints on their masculinity or femininity. The transition to school may thus involve the suspension or abandonment of previous understandings of masculinity or femininity as unworkable in the new situation. This can be an implicit or explicit process: Orbach (1993: 49) reports that her son, on finding that the other children in his class at school expressed their nervousness about entering the new setting through displays of violence, summed up his dilemma with the regretful comment that 'I'd like to be a gentle boy, Dad, but I just don't think I can manage it'.

Once their legitimacy as participants has been demonstrated, children have to establish their position in the community and, especially, within local power/knowledge configurations. How a child is positioned will of course vary over time and place, and there will be differences between specific sites within the classroom that are dominated by particular groups. Although some masculinities and femininities tend to be understood as more powerful than others, power/knowledge relations in the early years classroom, as everywhere else, are both fluid and open to challenge, resistance and subversion. Blaise (2005) gives a clear example of how this can operate, showing how a group of 'girly-girls', generally the most disparaged category even at this age (Browne 2004), was able to claim a moment of power in which they both controlled the position of other children in the nursery and resisted the attempts of the feminizt staff to undermine their expression, celebration and enforcement of dichotomous and gendered positions. She describes how one child, Penny, brought in clearly gender-coded plates for the children to use at her birthday tea party. The staff resisted this by putting out insufficient 'girl' plates for the number of girls, so that some would be forced to use 'boy' plates. Penny and her friend in turn subverted this strategy by instructing the other girls to sit only where there were 'girl' plates, even though some girls clearly thought that sitting with their friends was more important than having the 'correct' plate. They were supported in this by Penny's aunt, who supplied one girl in a 'boy' place with a replacement 'girl' plate. When another girl was forced to sit at an otherwise all-boy table, with a 'boy' plate, alongside the most dominant male, she was mocked by Penny and her friend. In this situation, Penny was able to use her understanding of her peers' dichotomous approach to gender, to manipulate the power/ knowledge relations in the classroom to her advantage. Not only was she able to control the seating choices of usually more powerful peers, she was able to subvert the staff's own attempts to undercut her traditional approach to femininity and masculinity as oppositionally constructed.

Establishing and maintaining legitimacy

Establishing oneself as a legitimate participant involves recognizing and performing what is seen as 'appropriate' for a boy or girl in the community of masculinity or femininity practice constructed, in this case, in a specific early years setting (Davies 1989). What this is will be shaped by factors both inside and outside the setting. Children come to nursery or school with their existing understandings of masculinity and femininity, developed in the communities of practice of which they have previously been members. They are also influenced by the values and perceptions of the adults in the setting, staff and peer conceptions of what is 'natural' behaviour, images from the media, and as they grow older, the structures of school. They use these, in conjunction with the perceptions of other newcomers and the constructions dominant within the peer group, to construct group understandings of the rules of being a 'proper' boy or girl in this context.

Both Skelton (2001) and Connolly (2004), studying young children in different parts of the United Kingdom, found that boys living in communities in which male violence was a part of daily life constructed and enacted aggressive masculinities in school. In particular, Connolly contrasts the 'internally expressed' masculinity of middle-class children from non-violent areas with an 'externally expressed' masculinity of those from poorer and more violent local communities. The former, he argues, is a masculinity focused on self-control and the display of specialist knowledge and skills, such as the ability to master particular computer games, while the latter is much more physically enacted, and centred (in his study) around the ability to perform wrestling moves and the strength to display them. These different forms of masculinity, he argues, are not simply a matter of choice for the children; they are embedded in the taken for granted worlds of their wider lives and so a fundamental part of their ways of being.

Although most writers focus on boys when considering the relationship between wider social groupings and the children's construction of localized masculinities and femininities, Woodward (2003: 123–4) also notes the influence of a close-knit and socially conservative community on girls' understanding of themselves and their future lives. Already by age 4, the girls in his study had decided that they would prefer to have female babies when they were older, because boys would be 'too bright and difficult', 'too rough', and 'too clever' for their future selves to cope with.

Children's communal constructions of masculinity and femininity are also influenced by those of the adults within the setting in which these constructions take place. In a Finnish study, Härkönen (1995) found that more than half of childcare personnel had traditional views of gender segregation at work, and brought this into their under-standings of work education. Woodward (2003) found that both teachers and children tended to give higher value to masculine-labelled activities, with one girl remarking that 'We get to play nice pussycats, the boys get to play exciting things' (Woodward 2003: 130). The teachers he studied also said that they preferred teaching boys 'because they were more active and interesting' (Woodward 2003: 179). Teachers in early years settings frequently use sex as a differentiator, saying that 'the girls' are sitting nicely, or threatening misbehaving boys with being seated among girls (Woodward 2003). They also tend both to blame and to punish boys more, for example, because they assume that it is the boys who are being noisy (Lloyd and Duveen 1992). Browne (2004: 106) notes that early years educators tend to describe both boys and girls in binary terms, perceiving boys as comparatively rough and boisterous, 'physical', 'competitive' and 'interested in exploring things', while girls are considered to be more sedate, 'chatty', 'eager to please' and 'calm and attentive'. As a result of this, there is a tendency to provide activities that boys are expected to enjoy, in order to keep them out of mischief (Woodward 2003). Connolly (1998) found that less well-behaved black boys, who were considered by staff to be particularly troublesome, were repeatedly praised for good behaviour as if it were unusual or unexpected, thus drawing attention to the staff's construction of them as naughty or unruly. Similarly, Skelton (2001) reports that boys considered to be difficult by teachers were given more chances to contribute in class than other children, sometimes to the extent that they dominated group oral work. Lloyd and Duveen (1992) further found that staff expectations of poor behaviour from boys were echoed by the children in the schools they studied.

Adults in early years settings also contribute to children's construc-tions of masculinity and femininity through their implicit and explicit understandings of what is 'natural' behaviour in young children. Walkerdine and the Girls and Mathematics Unit (1989) found that teachers' views of the 'naturalness' of young boys' sex talk led them to permit sexually abusive speech directed at both female nursery staff and girls. Browne (2004) argues that nursery staff's belief in children's 'need' for superhero play obscures the fact that it is almost exclusively undertaken by boys, allowing them to dominate large areas of play space in the demonstration of an aggressive and combative masculinity. Connolly (1998) further found that early years teachers' perceptions could be racialized, with staff in his study emphasizing the 'natural' sporting abilities of black children.

Woodward (2003: 180) notes that the teachers he worked with had different approaches to expressions of sexual and romantic attachment between boys and girls:

> Staff distinctly discouraged amorous relationships between pairs of boys, less so between girls and boys, and hardly at all between girls, revealing here, possibly unconsciously, a public homophobic attitude towards the boys while perhaps seeing the girls' behaviour in a non-sexual or sexually passive way.

Such differences are likely to have multitudinous effects, particularly in settings in which romantic attachment or sexual attractiveness are considered important aspects of masculinity or femininity, as will be discussed below.

Media images also play a role in young children's collective constructions of masculinity and femininity. Skelton and Hall (2001: 17) argue that 'the mass media, including toy and game manufacturers, are a continuing source of conventional gender stereotyping'. UK children's television programming still frequently includes competitions that pit groups of boys against groups of girls, emphasizing and reifying differences already constructed by children themselves. Television advertisements for children's toys are frequently designed to appeal specifically to boys or girls, reinforcing children's ideas about what is to be played with by each. As I write, a major UK supermarket chain has shelves labelled 'boys' toys' and 'girls' toys', with the former holding a wide variety of playthings, particularly those that involve physical activity, including frisbees, water guns, waveboards, cycling helmets, bats, balls and other outdoor equipment, and the latter mainly displaying dolls, soft toys and craft sets.

Within films, children's television programmes and popular fiction, superheroes, from Robin Hood to Superman, Spiderman and Power Rangers, are almost always male. Jordan (1995: 76) argues that 'the "warrior" discourse has a powerful hold on the imaginations of little boys', who use superhero play as a way of experiencing and enacting power. The emphasis on the hero as male is often reflected in the views of young children themselves. Browne (2004) found that, while boys did think women could be superheroes, they were hard put to name any, while girls argued that only boys could have superhero status. This remained the case even when they were presented with a clear role model in a children's story: several girls found it easier to identify with the girls and women being rescued, than with the female rescuer.

Conversely, the Barbie doll is marked as so quintessentially feminine (it has been found to be second only to make-up as a female-marked toy) that it can be used not only as a celebratory rallying image for girls, but also as a symbol of feminine pollution for boys. Messner (2000) describes how, in a Little League soccer tournament in the USA, a group of 5-year-old boys was so disturbed by a female team's celebration of 'girl power', centred around a Barbie symbol after which their team, the 'Barbie Girls' was named, that they invaded the girls' space and chased them away. Subsequently, he reports, the possibility of defeat by the Barbie Girls, if the boys failed to practise properly, was used by the latter's coach as a potent invocation of team unity.

School structures, and the taking up of positions in alignment with or against these, are also important for the construction of young children's individual and collective masculinities and femininities. Connolly (2004) argues that such positionings are classed, with middle-class children coming to school already accustomed to having their lives largely controlled by adults, in contrast to those from working-class families, who are accorded a significantly greater degree of freedom and responsibility. Jordan (1995: 77) notes that boys who resist the order of the kindergarten, while they are 'subjected to a variety of public humiliations ... as embryo "lads" and "bloods" ... have at their disposal a discourse in which "getting into trouble" at school has been elevated into a touchstone for masculinity'. Consequently, for some young children, the construction of masculinity, in particular, in opposition to the structures of schooling, is a powerful act of resistance that may be more personally rewarding than conformity.

It is thus clear that a variety of factors influence how masculinity and femininity are collectively constructed in specific early years classrooms. What become the dominant images of girlhood and boyhood will vary according to the setting and the specific influences that are brought to bear on it at any particular time. In considering the operation of communities of masculinity and femininity practice in early years classrooms, it is important to remember that schools are dynamic settings whose membership alters over time. Preschool nurseries in particular may have a frequently changing population, as children depart for compulsory schooling. Woodward (2003), researching in the

UK, where many districts maintain three annual entry points to mainstream schooling, notes that the departure of a dominant and socially conservative group of boys from the nursery after the Easter break had a significant effect on what was considered to be acceptable behaviour for boys, with an increased number playing in the home corner and with feminine-labelled toys such as dolls. Even the same setting, therefore, has a dynamic and constantly changing membership, which will in its turn have effects on what is considered most significant for local constructions of masculinity and femininity.

Constructing girlhood and boyhood

Young children construct girlhood and boyhood in strongly dichoto-mous ways. This is evident in early years classrooms, where the children's need to be clear about the boundaries between each community of practice, and to establish themselves as legitimate members, leads them to draw and enforce strong distinctions. The relational nature of gender is particularly salient here, with boundaries between boys and girls constructed through the Othering of the opposite sex (Paechter 1998), particularly on the part of boys, but also by girls. This takes place to the extent that objects labelled masculine may be experienced as polluting by girls, and vice versa. Blaise (2005) reports, for example, that in the tea party described earlier, children were reluctant to offer female staff members cake on 'boys' plates.

In such circumstances, where children are still uncertain about the constancy of gender but are clear about the necessity of claiming legitimate membership of one group or the other, the boundaries have to be drawn so starkly that evidence for their fluidity is discounted and ignored. Woodward (2003: 157) reports, for example, one boy as stating that 'daddy works and mummy doesn't', despite his mother being employed full-time. A boy in Davies's (1989) study denied vehemently that men wear skirts, although his Malaysian father wore sarongs:

> The fact that his father and his father's friend observably wore what could be called dresses needed to be ignored, or constructed as not fitting into the category of 'dress' in order to maintain not only the symbolic boundaries of the categories male and female, but their exclusiveness from each other.
>
> (Davies 1989: 20)

Similarly, Blaise (2005: 105) found that dominant boys were unable to acknowledge the recently demonstrated superior ability of the girls in their class at climbing a rope. When challenged about who had managed to reach the top, one of them simply reiterated, 'it was boys'.

The boundaries between the communities of masculinity and femininity practice in early years classrooms are further reinforced by the tendency of children at this age to play mainly in single-sex groups (Lloyd and Duveen 1992), and to focus on different activities in different spaces. The gendering of these spaces and the types of activities that take place in them combine to help both boys and girls feel powerful and secure in their identities, thus reinforcing their play preferences and further supporting the boundaries between them.

Boys have been found to have a particular propensity to engage in superhero play (Lloyd and Duveen 1992). This is supported by media images in which superheroes are almost invariably male, to the extent that, when presented with a female superhero, boys ignore her gender (Davies 1989). Browne (2004: 92) points out that:

> Superhero play is essentially a display of hegemonic masculinity, and therein lies the appeal for some boys. Recurring episodes of superhero play enable boys to experience repeatedly a specific type of masculine power and the emotional high that goes with this experience of power.

That is not to say that girls are always unable or unwilling to take such power for themselves when it is offered in such a way that it will be accessible to them. Marsh (2000) argues that when a superhero discourse is presented to children that includes positive images of women as active agents, then girls become very interested in superhero narratives. She found, however, that in their superhero stories and role plays, girls tended to place Batwoman in a supportive role to Batman, and that where she operated autonomously, it was usually to rescue children and old women. Meanwhile, the boys never mentioned Batwoman at all, and generally resisted the girls' desire to take part in superhero play.

The working-class boys studied by Connolly (2004) in Northern Ireland took this focus on males as strong, powerful heroes further. Their play emphasized wrestling moves and practising fighting: having ability and strength in wrestling conferred status. Both superhero play and mock fighting are highly visible and take up a large area, establishing a male spatial dominance in the playground that continues into mainstream schooling, as discussed in Chapter 7. This further reinforces them as important signifiers of powerful masculinities. The performance of masculinity through superhero and fighting play is a public assertion of the right to take up and control space to the exclusion of others which reflects adult male dominance of public arenas (Massey 1994).

As discussed earlier, neither boys nor girls find it easy to consider females as possible candidates for superhero status. Although Marsh's work suggests that girls can successfully be included, the girls in Davies's (1989) research found it hard even to imagine themselves as strong enough to be superheroes. One boy in Browne's (2004) study argued that, when girls wanted to be strong, they could be mothers, and this is in effect what happens. The home corner is an unquestionably female domain, inhabited almost exclusively by girls playing mummies and babies, with the occasional boy as a subordinated daddy, child or dog. Woodward (2003) did find a few boys who occasionally played mummies and daddies with each other, and one boy in Davies's (1989) study sometimes played in the home corner alone. Generally, however, boys who want to join in with family- and household-focused play have to do so on the girls' terms.

Girls of this age use domestic play as a way of feeling powerful. The image of the powerful woman in the home is a potent one for young children (Davies 1989; Walkerdine and The Girls and Mathematics Unit 1989), and girls in the role of 'mummy' enact this to the full, bossing their 'children' and 'husband' about and generally revelling in being in charge. This experience of female power through domestic play, however, has strongly negative aspects. It confines them to a small and enclosed area of the nursery, and gives them a very limited range of roles, the majority of which are subordinate: in most play families, there is only one mummy. For boys, while these games can clearly be highly satisfying (Davies 1989), they are also risky. Although Browne (2004) argues that some boys are able to adhere to hegemonic forms of masculinity in enough respects to be able to take part in female-labelled play without losing status, for others this is not possible. Woodward (2003), for example, describes a boy dressing and undressing a doll under the table, one eye constantly over his shoulder to check whether he was being observed by the other boys.

Children use their bodies in a number of ways to demonstrate their membership of communities of masculinity and femininity practice. How the body is held, how it is moved, the actions carried out, are all used to delineate, perform and reinforce masculinity or femininity, so that in a short time real bodily differences emerge as a result in variations in use (Bourdieu 2001; Young 2005). Different physical practices result in different amounts of muscle, fluency of movement and confidence in the use of one's body, a continually reinforcing spiral of physical difference. Such distinctions may also be supported and reinforced by staff and by other children, for example, by reminding girls to sit demurely (Woodward 2003). These injunctions reinforce and amplify the effects of differential parental handling that are already established in the first years of life, producing increasingly distinct male and female bodies.

Membership of communities of masculinity and femininity practice is also demonstrated through how the body is clothed. For boys, this is moderately straightforward: they do not wear skirts or dresses. There are also some colours and patterns, notably pink, and flowery fabrics (though others may emerge from time to time in different settings) which are linked with femininity: for boys of this age, the prime mode of demonstrating masculinity through attire concerns the avoidance of anything labelled as feminine. For girls, the situation can be more complex, as different femininities are expressed through clothing styles. Blaise (2005: 61–2) notes clear differences between the dress codes of those the children referred to as 'girly-girls' and those considered to be 'cool':

> Being a girly-girl means wearing frilly, ruffly, and cute outfits, with matching shoes, tights, and barrettes or ribbons. Pink is a desirable color for this look ... Cool girls achieve their look by wearing clothes considered to be the latest in fashion, such as bell-bottom pants, Spice Girl logos, baseball caps turned backward, and the color black.

For some children, make-up is a key marker of femininity, even at age 4, though they do seem to make a distinction between 'play' make-up, which is permitted by their mothers, and 'real' make-up, which is not (Blaise 2005). Blaise found that some girls were fascinated by make-up, seeing it as important for looking beautiful and attracting boys. Because of its strong feminine marking (Messner 2000), make-up has to be anathema to young boys wanting to preserve their legitimate membership of the local community of masculinity practice. This is made clear to them in a number of ways. Blaise (2005) recounts an incident in which a boy showed an excited interest in the make-up that a girl had brought into school. The 'inappropriateness' of his behaviour was demonstrated by the girl ignoring his questions, disgusted body language from another boy, and laughter from the class. Blaise (2005: 76–7) argues that:

> this group of young children works hard at letting Cheng know that his interest in makeup is not 'normal' for boys. By not allowing Cheng to venture into the feminine realm, or by making it difficult for him to do so, the children are actively regulating the gendered social order of their class and supporting the heterosexual matrix.

Cheng's interest in the make-up calls into question not only his own masculinity but also, by association, that of the other boys. It also challenges the children's understanding of make-up as quintessentially feminine. Such underminings of the already tenuously established social order are too much for the children to cope with, and they make it clear to Cheng that such interests are not acceptable in boys.

Children also use dressing-up clothes as part of their construction of masculinities and femininities within early years classrooms. Davies (1989) notes that some items of clothing can be imbued with symbolic power, and adopted or discarded accordingly. She reports one girl putting on a man's waistcoat in order to retrieve a doll from a boy who had snatched it, discarding it once victorious, while a boy was observed to remove a black velvet skirt in the middle of a fight, as part of his strategy for winning. Children police others' play dress almost as much as their everyday clothing. They label items as 'for girls' and 'for boys', and cross-dressing, even to a limited degree, can make them very uneasy, particularly if it involves boys wearing dresses (Skelton and Hall 2001). Woodward (2003: 165) notes how newcomers' 'mistakes' regarding dressing-up can be contested forcibly by old-timers in the local communities of masculinity and femininity practice. In this case, the boys are protecting male prerogatives:

> Carola ... put on a police tabard and a policeman's hat. Jeremy ... and Roger ... forcefully informed her that she had the wrong hat on, and that only boys were allowed to wear that hat! Duncan ... then roughly seized the hat Carola was wearing and ran and returned with a lady police officer's hat, and menacingly told her to wear it!

Carola's appropriation of a symbol of masculine authority is too much for these dominant boys to bear, and she is shown in no uncertain terms that it is unacceptable.

Children between 3 and 6 frequently construct masculinities and femininities as dichotomous through a (hetero)sexualized boyfriend–girlfriend culture. This varies between settings and between social class groups. Scott (2002) notes that in one early years class she studied, the African-American girls were fascinated by the African-American boys, and named individuals among them as boyfriends. Connolly (1998) found that in a predominantly working-class British setting, conflicts between black and white 5–6-year-old boys revolved around 'ownership' of high-status white girls, with fights breaking out between the boys as a result. He notes that:

Girlfriends appeared to play a significant role for many boys in relation to the development and maintenance of their masculinity within the field of masculine peer-group relations. Inasmuch as girls were therefore centrally constructed as symbolic markers of territory through the conflicts over girlfriends, then it was inevitable that they came to be both objectified and sexualized by the boys.

(Connolly 1998: 106)

This objectification of the girls meant that there was a clear distinction for these boys, though not for all in their class, between having girlfriends, which was a strong marker of masculinity, and having girls as friends, which undermined this, and so was avoided. While the white girls were claimed as possessable sex objects, in the same school, South Asian girls were positioned as a sexual Other by both boys and girls from other ethnic groups: they were seen as sensual, erotic, mysterious and unpredictable, even at age 5.

For a girl, having a boyfriend may bring prestige (Blaise 2005), making her, as a desirable female, an unassailable member of the local community of heterosexually constructed femininity practice. However, this comes at a price. Boyfriend–girlfriend relations in early years settings involve the Othering of girls within a ruthlessly heterosexualized framework that leaves little room for flexibility in how they perform their femininities.

Conclusion

For newcomers in early years classrooms, encountering a new community without parental support for possibly the first time, the establishment of legitimate participation is fundamental to their ability to operate within the local communities of masculinity and femininity practice. Gender is so salient to young children, as a way of ordering the world, that establishing oneself as a 'proper' boy or girl in the new setting is of paramount importance. As with other aspects of behaviour, young children expect to gather clues as to what is, and what is not, acceptable, from the adults and other children they encounter. They expect them to guide and correct their behaviour, so that it conforms to what is expected as a competent performance of 'boy' or 'girl' in that context. They are not disappointed. Both adults and children make these expectations known, in subtle and not-so-subtle ways.

These expectations can be quite specific to the setting and can conflict with those in other places, for example at home, and children are also aware of this. Woodward (2003), for example, notes that during a period in which doll play was considered anathema for boys dominating the community of masculinity practice in the nursery he studied, some of the younger boys continued to play openly with dolls at home. Conversely, the girl in Blaise's study, who brought in gender-coded plates for her party, will have been aware that the staff in the nursery understood boys and girls as being much more similar than did the adults at home; her ability to subvert and resist the nursery staff's intentions is partly due to her knowledge of this and the support that she got from family members in making and marking difference in her preparations for the party.

Once legitimacy has been established, it has to be maintained. This involves continuing to demonstrate that one knows the rules of the game, that one understands what boys can do and what is only for girls, and vice versa. As participation continues, this may allow one to have more influence on what is considered an acceptable performance: Woodward (2003) notes, for example, that changes in the population of the nursery he studied allowed previously subordinate boys to establish that they might play with dolls without compromising their masculinity. While young children constantly erect and reinforce borders between boys and girls, those boundaries remain fluid, subject to alteration over time and as changes occur in the population of the early years classroom.

The maintenance of difference between boys and girls requires a wide array of performances. 'Borderwork' (Thorne 1993) among children of this age involves distinctions in dress, play preference, space use and bodily comportment as well as the Othering of the opposite sex, particularly of girls by boys, through objectified (hetero)sexualized relationships. All of these construct and reinforce boundaries between boys and girls in a strongly oppositional process through which some of the activities, preoccupations and symbols of the other sex come to be seen as polluting.

The borders between masculinity and femininity are constructed so strongly at this age because gender constancy is not yet well established. Children are not sure whether, if they behave like one of the other sex, if they appear to be a member of the 'wrong' community of practice, they will actually find they belong there. As they grow older and understand that they will not change their sex with their behaviour, such strong dualisms become more relaxed. At this point, however, other factors, more specific to schooling, start to come into play. It is these that we will examine in the next chapter.

Interventions

Children aged 3–6, as we have seen, tend to construct masculinity and femininity in strongly oppositional terms, with rigid barriers between the two. Their uncertainty about gender constancy, and their need to establish themselves as legitimate members of child communities of masculinity and femininity practice, mean that they find it hard to think and talk about masculinities and femininities as being in any way fluid or overlapping. They will also ignore evidence contrary to the absoluteness of their views. Consequently, it has proven difficult to intervene in young children's constructions of masculinities and femininities. Boys may ignore the sex of female superheroes in feminizt stories, while girls may find it hard to identify with them; both sexes are likely to criticize princesses who fail to behave in suitably 'princess-like' ways (Davies 1989). Attempts to give counter-examples to stereotypical views may simply fall flat. It is also important to be aware that some feminizt interventions may be experienced as disempowering by some children; Blaise (2005) suggests that this may well have been the case for the girl who ended up with a 'boy' plate at the tea party described in this chapter.

Nevertheless, there are some things that can be attempted:

- Before intervening, observe what is going on in the specific setting that you intend to intervene in; settings can vary enormously. Be aware that the same setting can change over time, particularly if it is a nursery from which children regularly depart for mainstream school.
- Treat superhero play with caution and recognize its limitations. In particular, do not let it take over the whole of the outdoor play space, marginalizing other activities.
- Take care with your own language and ensure that you do not reinforce boundaries between boys and girls. For example, name those you are reprimanding or praising, rather than referring to 'the girls' or 'the boys'.
- Actively support girls and boys taking part in activities that the local communities of masculinity and femininity practice construct as being for the other sex.
- Provide books with a range of role models and discuss them with the children, but do not be too disappointed if they fail to identify with or follow them.
- Discourage the objectification of girls through the girlfriend/ boyfriend culture. If necessary, point out explicitly that no one 'owns' anyone else.
- Finally, remember that small changes are still changes.

6   Boys and girls in primary schools

And yet, painful as was this fresh overthrow of her pride, it was neither the worst nor the most lasting result of the incident. This concerned her schoolfellows. By the following morning the tale of her doings was known to everyone. It was circulated in the first place, no doubt, by Lilith Gordon, who bore her a grudge for her offer to accompany the song: had Laura not put herself forward in this objectionable way, Lilith might have escaped singing altogether. Lilith also resented her having shown that she could do it – and this feeling was generally shared. It evidenced want of good-fellowship and made you very glad the little prig had afterwards come to grief: if you had abilities that others had not, you concealed them, instead of parading them under other people's noses.

(Richardson 1981: 82–3)

Introduction

For children aged between about 5–6 and 11–12, primary or elementary schooling is a major site for the construction of communities of masculinity and femininity practice. First, and most simply, it is where other children are encountered in significant numbers. These include older children, who may be treated as more central members of such communities and who can act as indicators of the staging posts on the journey towards full membership of adult communities. At the same time, however, the social world of the classroom is not the same as that of the playground discussed in Chapter 7, and the masculinities and femininities constructed in each may have significant differences. Thorne (1993) points out that boys and girls are more likely to play with each other in local neighbourhoods than they are in school: the different situation, in which, among other things, there are fewer friends to choose from, breaks down the binaries that are held to so strongly in other arenas. Even in school, classroom and playground relations will be subtly different as varying power/knowledge configurations and spatial and bodily relationships come to the fore.

Other features of the school setting make it a very particular site for the construction of masculinities and femininities. It contains adults who are in a specific relation to the children: they have a formal, quasi-parental but, above all, educative role, and they may come from a different social, ethnic and class background from that of the children they teach. Thus, they may be part of local communities of masculinity and femininity practice, or they may be outside of them, with the children constructing their own communities partly in opposition to those of the teachers. Schooling also deals in knowledge forms that, even in the primary years, are differentially labelled as masculine and feminine and therefore as impacting on local communities of masculinity and femininity practice in different ways. Finally, school is an institution that, by its very nature, selects, labels and sorts children. The groupings imposed by the school, and indeed the very fact of this continuous classification, encourage ways of thinking about the self and others that involve understandings about who is supposed to be in which configuration and who is not. They emphasize sameness and difference, and foreground issues of legitimacy.

The masculinities and femininities collectively constructed by children in schools are formed in relation to the school-based peer group; older children; school as a disciplinary institution and spatial site producing and purveying knowledge; and children's individual and collective understanding of the other inhabitants of that site. Masculinities and femininities are not, therefore, developed by the peer group and imposed onto the classroom: classroom and institutional processes are of key importance in their construction. There are also close relationships between school communities of masculinity and femininity practice and those that arise in more peer-dominated settings; they influence and interact with each other, though they are not the same.

Classroom-based masculinities and femininities are also formed in a situation in which children are expected to construct themselves not just as boys and girls but, overwhelmingly, as pupils. This will have the dual effects of repressing extreme conceptions of masculinity and femininity and of introducing resistance as a factor in these constructions. Some classroom-based masculinities and femininities will be constructed through resistance, others through conformity, to the pupil role. Warrington *et al.* (2003) argue that some boys bring to school notions of masculinity that are in direct conflict with the ethos of the school and pupilhood. They report that some boys spoke of having to pretend a lack of interest and involvement in school work in order to preserve their status in the peer group. The contradictions between being a successful pupil and being a full member of a local community of masculinity (or femininity) practice that is constructed in opposition to this can be very strong. They can be particularly problematic for boys, however: compliant pupilhood, as a subordinate position, is generally understood as feminine.

The masculinities and femininities that are constructed in primary classrooms are not unitary, but multiple and relationally understood. They can be seen to constitute overlapping communities of masculinity and femininity practice that are explicitly and implicitly defined against each other through inclusion and exclusion. The interdependent aspect of the construction of these communities is extremely important, and operates on at least two levels. First, femininities of all kinds are overwhelmingly defined as the excluded Other of masculinity: the relation between them is dualistic rather than one of equal opposites (Paechter 1998). This allows masculinity itself to be invisible, with an assumption that to be a person is to be male (Kessler and McKenna 1978). Walkerdine (1984) argues that this is indeed the case for the active, exploring, Piagetian child central to many conceptions of primary education, and that this results in the undervaluing of girls' achievements. It may, however, happen also with the children themselves. Davies (2003) argues that boys are more likely to define themselves as persons and as not-girls than as boys, while girls specifically consider their girlhood as part of identity. On the other hand, boys exhibit a striving for masculinity that arises from their peripherality as members of adult communities of masculinity practice. It is possibly not so much that their masculinity is invisible, as that they aspire for it to be so.

Second, particular forms of masculinity and femininity in specific classrooms are also constructed in relation to each other. Renold (2001), in a British study, describes a group of 'square-girls' for whom a major aspect of their collective identity was the rejection of things that were central to the femininities of other girls in the class. These high-achieving girls, who were positively oriented towards academic achievement and strongly rejected the heterosexual narratives of the wider classroom culture, understood themselves in highly oppositional terms, making a clear separation between their own group and the other girls: 'Although to be "square" signified a particularly feminized position, it also involved differentiating themselves from dominant feminine performances, evidenced by their lack of interest in street fashion and the popular pursuit of boys as potential boyfriends' (Renold 2001: 578). All school masculinities and femininities, however, both dominant and subordinate, are influenced and bound up with schooling as a site for the construction and arena for the performance of identities. I will, therefore, in this chapter, be looking at the ways in which the disciplines, practices and spaces of primary schooling interact with, support and undermine the development of certain forms of masculinity and femininity practice.

It is important to bear in mind that communities of masculinity and femininity practice are very much local constructions. Different masculinities and femininities will be constructed as dominant and marginal in different settings and situations and, as we saw in Chapter 3, their relationships may change over time. Such constructions will be oppositional to each other or to schooling to different degrees and in different ways, depending both on the situation within the school itself and on what the children concerned bring to it. Swain (2005: 81) reports, for example, on an elite private primary school where, in contrast to the others in his study, 'the great majority of boys ... did not feel the need to secure their sense of "maleness" by traducing all things feminine and female as the foundation of their masculinity was relatively stable, confident, and secure.' Connolly (2004) contrasts working-class masculinities in one school he studied, which were constructed in opposition to girls, with middle-class masculinities in another school that positioned themselves against both girls and working-class boys; Skelton (2001) suggests that such middle-class masculinities may be supported and encouraged by teachers as part of an assertion and encouragement of a school-based group identity.

In all of these constructions, race, class, and geographical and cultural locations will have important effects. Nevertheless, there seem to be some commonalities to the ways in which communities of masculinity and femininity practice develop in the school setting. First, boys have a tendency to construct some form of 'muscular masculinity': ways of being that require the public flexing of real or metaphorical muscles as part of a demonstration of their maleness. This may involve performances of either physical or mental prowess, according to the situation (Redman and Mac an Ghaill 1997). Second, it seems to be extremely difficult for girls to construct femininities that involve publicly celebrating, enjoying, or even taking ownership of their academic achievement, without a strong risk of permanent peripherality.

The control of bodies in school

Children's bodies are strongly and multiply regulated within school spaces. This is partly because the dualistic understandings of the self, discussed in Chapter 2, require the mind to be separated from the body for the purposes of learning. Because the emphasis is on the education of the mind (despite some lip service paid to the idea of the healthy body

(Paechter 2004)), the Cartesian mind/body split requires children's bodies to be sidelined, if not erased, for the purposes of education. This means that a considerable part of the energy of the schooling system has to go into disciplining and confining children's bodies, so that they cannot interfere with the main purposes of schooling, which are to do with the mind. Consequently, as Foucault (1978) has pointed out, children's bodies, and children's sexualities, are both ubiquitous and denied within the school system. School buildings are organized in such a way that surveillance is possible at more or less any time; there is very little privacy for the children (Foucault 1977; Markus 1996).

Children's bodies are particularly closely regulated in classrooms where, after all, the mind is supposed to be being trained. Although they are no longer arranged formally in rank order (Markus 1996), where they sit, and with whom, is still closely organized and regulated in many schools. Children may be grouped according to ability for teaching purposes, or seated in ability groups within a supposed mixed ability classroom, cutting across self-chosen groupings. In recent years some schools in the UK have adopted a policy of seating students in boy–girl pairs (Ivinson and Murphy 2003), to form a regime that expects some students (usually the girls) to regulate the behaviour of the others; this both controls the children's bodies and constructs boys and girls as different across a 'silly/sensible' dichotomy (Francis 1998) that seems to be pervasive in primary schools. Even curriculum forms can impact directly on children's bodies. The National Literacy and Numeracy Strategies for England (Department for Education and Employment 1998a, 1998b) require considerable periods of whole class teaching; for children under 8 this usually takes place squashed together cross-legged, without fidgeting, on a carpeted area of the classroom. Children's bodies are thus brought together for group surveillance and control so that their minds can be communally improved.

This bodily regulation constrains children in different ways. As we saw in Chapters 4 and 5, girls have had less encouragement, since birth, to be strongly physically active, and by the time they reach primary school they are already used to having to consider how they dress and move in the interest of 'decency'. Middle-class children are more used to physical regulation (Connolly 2004) so may not be as consciously aware of, and therefore resistant to, the confining aspects of schooling. Furthermore, teachers expect boys to be unable to sit still (Jones and Myhill 2004b), and treat them accordingly. Jones and Myhill (2004a) report that boys are more likely to be seen by teachers as fidgety, immature and having poor behaviour and motivation than are girls. Warrington et al. (2003) argue that such differences in teachers' perception are noticed by children, who believe that teachers have differential expectations of boys' and girls' behaviour, the quality of their written work, and the reasons for which they might be punished.

All of these varying reactions to the bodily regulation of schooling come together to affect boys' and girls' understanding of themselves, individually and in groups, and of each other. Their perceptions of what teachers think about them will further influence their beliefs about the extent to which they will be able to get away with resistance, and so be self-reinforcing. If boys, for example, believe that they are less likely than girls to be punished for failing always to keep their bodies within the bounds prescribed by the school, they will also be less likely to try to conform to these requirements, further developing the communal construction of boys as less able to keep their bodies in check than girls.

Bodily regulation in the classroom is also related to a distinction reported by Francis (1998) in UK research with primary age children. She argues that girls are seen by both teachers and children as sensible and selfless, boys as silly and selfish:

> Of the feminine construction, maturity, obedience and neatness are the valued 'sensible' qualities, which naturally lead to 'selflessness' – giving and facilitating. The masculine construction involves 'silly' qualities of immaturity, messiness and naughtiness, leading to 'selfishness' – taking and demanding.
> (Francis 1998: 40)

She argues that the sensible/selfless position is taken up as powerful by girls in single-sex groups, where it benefits from the approval of other girls. In mixed groups, however, it can lead to abandonment of power to boys, who will use the silly/selfish position to prevent any activity taking place at all if it does not work to their advantage. Such positionings, she suggests, can prevent boy only groups from functioning. Hey *et al.* (2001), however, note that social class has a bearing on this duality of constructions. While British working-class girls will follow their teachers in understanding boys' disruptive behaviour as being the result of individual difficulties and therefore in need of care and consideration, middle-class girls do not:

> In the particular learning ethos of Trafnell Park, girls take their cue from their teachers and are compelled to reconsider aspects of boys' 'disruption' as psychological 'disturbance'. After all, the dominant discourse (especially for working-class girls) assumes and rewards a caring femininity – and obversely punishes the withdrawal of caring. Girls rescue boys from themselves and (like

their teacher) to that extent are disarmed from further critical insights.

(Hey *et al.* 2001: 131)

Powerful middle-class girls in a different school, on the other hand, dismissed as risible their male peers' attempts to construct dominant disruptive masculinities. They treated the boys with dismissive exasperation and set out (successfully) to compete with them academically. The result was 'moaning, sulking, moodiness or anger' (Hey *et al.* 2001: 132) on the part of the boys. Hey *et al.* (2001: 133) argue that:

> Boys resent girls looking out for themselves rather than for them. This can intensify the oppositions between 'sensible' girls and 'non-sensible' boys and is likely to reproduce highly gender-differentiated behaviours with consequences for schooling outcomes.

Thus, while differential expectations of physical and other behaviour are likely to lead to greater divergence between boys and girls as they are treated differently, when girls instead take up stereotypically masculine stances, this also reinforces difference through the oppositional reaction of boys.

Bodies as problems: the erasure of sexualities in primary schooling

The regulation of bodies in schools is related to the denial of children's sexualities in this and other arenas. Such a denial arises from a combination of the valorization of the rational within school knowledge (Paechter 2004) and the myth of childhood innocence (Bhana 2002), so that the idea that children might have feeling, emotional bodies disappears. Consequently, the expectation of the school is that children construct disembodied masculinities and femininities, despite the way that schooling constantly draws attention to children's bodies by regulating and segregating them. Such disembodied identities are, of course, impossible, but even attempting to comply with this requirement is easier for some groups of children than for others. Renold (2001: 578) notes that the 'square-girls' she studied were singled out for their 'perceived obsession with the mind over the body' and their lack of interest in fashion and physical appearance. Their academic femininities were in many ways constructed in opposition to the resistant femininities of the other girls in the class, who worked hard to retain a place for their bodies in school.

Many middle-class boys construct communities of masculinity practice around an idea of 'mental muscularity' which emphasizes intellectual rather than physical gymnastics (Redman and Mac an Ghaill 1997), the ability to sustain an argument and, often, confidence with technology. Such masculinities are valued by schools (Skelton and Francis 2003), suggesting that it may still be these children for whom school is ultimately designed. Gallas (1998) notes that in her classroom it was these highly articulate, white, middle-class boys who were able to challenge the teacher and dominate other children by using language in a sophisticated way to control social interactions. At the same time, the practices of 'good girl' femininity, because they involve controlling the body and holding it in check, can similarly be understood as disembodied, in conformity to the wishes of the school.

Thus, in most cases, children's bodies are an absent presence in school. Where they do have a place, it is in physical education, where as Williams (1993) points out, masculine-labelled competitive sports are likely to predominate, reinforcing particular constructions of masculinity and sidelining the female body altogether. Apart from this, bodies only appear as part of resistance strategies, breaking through the regulation to assert physical masculinities or sexual femininities in the face of erasure.

Teachers' masculinities and femininities

Teachers are not members of child communities of masculinity and femininity practice, but, as members of local adult communities, they can influence children's collective constructions. This can happen through the performance or validation of particular forms of masculinity or femininity, or by calling these explicitly or implicitly into question. The relationship between teachers' and children's performances and constructions of masculinity and femininity will be strongly influenced by social class, and be affected, at least in part, by the extent to which teachers themselves consider the children they teach to be similar to, or different from, them.

Both Connolly (2004) and Skelton (2001) report that the teachers in the violent working-class communities they studied saw local adults as childlike and unable to support their children effectively, and considered that the values of the school and the home were significantly different. Rather than attempt to act as models of alternative masculinities and femininities for the children, both male and female teachers adopted a masculine, aggressive, physically intimidating disciplinary stance, intended to keep order and minimize disruption, believing that it was necessary to socialize the children to the mores of the school before academic learning could take place (Skelton 2001). Given the teachers' understanding of the children and their families as essentially Other, it is unlikely that the children would find much to identify with in their performances of masculinity and femininity.

Between male teachers and middle-class boys, on the other hand, there can be a strong sense of identification. Skelton (2001) argues that, in a culture in which elementary school teaching is positioned as women's work, male teachers preserve their masculine identities by locating themselves with the boys they teach. In the middle-class British school she studied, the dominant masculinity 'was reminiscent of an exclusive male sports club where members bond through shared humour and shared commitments to, and interests in, "their" sport' (Skelton 2001: 128). Some teachers performed a 'laddish' masculinity which was aligned with that of the boys they taught and involved the marginalization and teasing of girls, especially through the mutual valorization of football. Girls were thus communally positioned as Other through the demonstration and masculinization of privileged football knowledge. In such situations, male teachers are attempting to position themselves as 'old-timer' members of the community of masculinity practice constructed by the boys in the class. This is part of their resistance to inclusion, or even resentment at their peripherality, as males, in the feminized local community of practice of primary school teachers. Such positionings may be in many ways themselves oppositional in relation to the school: Skelton (2001) reports that their manifestations included the open undermining of equity education.

Conversely, female primary teachers have a tendency to identify with 'good girls' as being not particularly able but achieving through hard work (Walkerdine and The Girls and Mathematics Unit 1989). This both undervalues girls' success and constructs clever girls as subteachers, supporting boys and other girls (Lucey *et al.* 2003). Walden and Walkerdine (1985) argue that the sub-teacher role is one in which girls are allowed to be both feminine and academically successful; its association with 'being nice' and supporting others gives some girls space to be seen as clever, because their success is being used in the service of others. On the other hand, it feeds into the dualistic ethos of girls as 'sensible selfless' helpers (Francis 1998; Hey *et al.* 2001), in contraposition of the silliness and helplessness of less able boys.

Teachers' beliefs about children and about the world also influence what counts as 'normal' in any particular classroom. Martino *et al.* (2004) suggest that many teachers think of gender and schooling in terms of normalizing assumptions that essentialize particular ways of behaving for boys and girls. This leads teachers, they argue, to modify their pedagogies in gendered ways which then reinforce their expectations about how children think, behave and learn. In particular, this allows the legitimation of gender regimes in which certain versions of masculinity (such as those focused around physical activity) are reinscribed within the classroom. Teachers have been found to have strongly binary beliefs regarding children, making clear distinctions between what they expect boys and girls to be like (Jones and Myhill 2004b). Such beliefs are likely to influence what masculinities and femininities can be constructed in their classrooms.

Teachers' assumptions regarding heterosexuality can also influence what forms of masculinity and femininity practice can be constructed in their classrooms. Benjamin (2003) demonstrates that the assumption of heterosexuality can be challenged even within an overwhelmingly macho and misogynistic culture, but in practice such challenges are only made by a few committed teachers. Indeed, in Skelton's (2001) study, male teachers were at pains to demonstrate their own heterosexual masculinities, and did so through sexually objectifying banter that included the boys but embarrassed the girls. While the latter did find a number of ways to resist this, including making fun of the teacher for his casual mode of dress, the only girl who mounted an explicit challenge was perceived by both teachers and other children as unfeminine. Such examples make it clear that it is possible for children's masculinities and femininities to be strongly constrained by the needs and desires of teachers to construct their own identities in particular ways.

Masculinities, femininities and school knowledge

Masculinities and femininities are also constructed by children in relation to school knowledge. Although this relationship is not as strong as it is in secondary schooling, there is still some evidence that younger children position themselves, at least in part, according to their perceptions of some school-based knowledges as masculine or feminine. Davies (2003) argues that, in the primary school classroom, teachers assume the ownership of knowledge, and that children are actively taught to defer to the teacher and to textual authority. Harris (1999) argues that this is especially the case in poorer countries, where textbooks continue to represent the access route to high-status knowledge. This means that in their content and layout they can address groups of pupils selectively through their approaches to pedagogy. She notes that there is masculine bias in primary mathematics texts in both

India and Bangladesh, and that this is both of indigenous origin (for example, through traditional stories) and the result of colonial importation. Similarly, Jackson and Gee (2005) argue that illustrations in school readers in New Zealand continue to represent girls and women differently from boys and men. In particular, even in feminizt texts, girls are drawn holding objects close to their bodies, a clear marker of femininity (Goffman 1976). Boys, on the other hand, are shown holding objects away from their bodies, even when these objects are those labelled as feminine, such as dolls.

Despite recent arguments that primary schools are feminized arenas (Skelton 2002), a masculine competitive ethos is fostered in many schooling systems through the increased emphasis on testing in national and state curricula (Paechter 2007). Such emphases foreground approaches to knowledge that focus on the rational and disembodied, with a valorization of a mentally muscular masculinity that, for example, emphasizes the public performance of educational competence over the private practice of it. Lucey *et al.* (2003: 50) give an example in which a 7-year-old girl is forced, through the organizational structures of English primary mathematics, publicly to perform competence and hard work, despite clearly having no idea what she is doing:

> As part of a whole class session, the teacher is working on halving numbers. Each child has an individual white board and marker pen with which to display numbers.
>
> Teacher: Half of 36?
>
> Meg starts to lift her board up to show the teacher. She has written '15', but before she shows it she notices that others around her have '18'. She quickly changes it; the teacher does not notice and says, 'Well done, Meg.'
>
> Teacher: Half of 72?
>
> Meg puts on an act. She takes the top off her pen, pushes it back again and looks puzzled. She appears to be counting – her lips are moving but it is not clear what she is saying. She turns round and sees what George has written then turns back again and wrinkles her face (as if to say, 'I'm concentrating hard'). Then she looks round at several boards and sees what answer others have got. Next she closes her eyes and screws up her face. After a time her face lights up as if she's just made a big discovery and she writes down '36'.

As a girl who wants to present herself in class as competent and hard-working, Meg cannot afford to be seen to be floundering. The practices of the classroom combine with the mores of the local community of femininity practice to prevent her from learning; not drawing attention to oneself through incompetence becomes more important than achieving understanding.

Classroom practices in which children are required publicly to demonstrate competence or, especially, high performance are problematic for both boys and girls, but in different ways. Warrington *et al.* (2003) argue that, while high-achieving boys are generally found to enjoy competition, the association of masculinity with success means that a competitive classroom atmosphere – often encouraged because teachers believe that it is more 'boy-friendly' (Bhana 2002) – may actually do less successful boys a disservice. Faced with competition, they may give up and try to perform their masculinity in other ways (Skelton and Francis 2003). Even where such an ethos is not directly encouraged, some of the everyday practices of schooling may have this effect. Silent reading, for example, while ostensibly private, is in many ways an extremely public activity when it takes place in the classroom (Gallas 1998). Children can see what everyone is reading and, if this includes graded reading books, its level of difficulty. Moss and Attar (1999) suggest that 7–11 year old boys who are not proficient readers deal with this situation by choosing impressively big, but picture filled, reference books and spending the time examining the pictures rather than reading the text. Thus they appear to their peers to be reading appropriately difficult books, while, in practice, doing no reading at all, leading to a vicious circle of poor performance which has continually to be protected from exposure to the ridicule of other boys.

Girls, on the other hand, are under considerable pressure from their peers to play down and diminish their academic success. This is related to the way that girl communities of femininity practice tend to treat being 'nice' as an essential part of acceptable femininity. Although what constitutes niceness varies between groups of girls, it seems to be a theme that runs through many accounts of schoolgirl femininities. Kehily *et al.* (2002: 171) note that a central criterion of belonging for the predominantly South-East Asian 9–10-year-olds they studied was that a girl 'should be nice, even when scorned, be truthful and be consistently well behaved'. These girls were strongly critical of another who, while conforming in class, made fun of other children in the playground. Generally, 'nice' girls are expected to work hard and behave well both in class and in the playground, and not to assert themselves, play aggressively (Evaldson 2003), or take pride in their academic achievement (Renold 2001). Hey (1997), researching slightly older girls, suggests that the public suppression of disagreement is of fundamental importance; to be positioned as assertive and bossy can lead to exclusion from the group because 'being disagreeable (bossy and thus openly assertive) was the exact antithesis of niceness' (Hey 1997: 56) and, as was suggested of one girl in her study, such behaviour 'undermined her claims to be suitably "nice"' (Hey 1997: 65). Walkerdine *et al.* (2001) argue that the salience of niceness has its origins in middle-class mothering practices, as part of a strategy in which power relations between mother and daughter are masked by appeals to a child's rationality and an illusion of autonomy on the part of the child:

> Strong emotional responses are discouraged, just as powerful emotions are converted into rational argument. Powerful emotions have to be expressed as nice or not nice feelings. In this way girls can be both feminine and avoid what is understood as the worst excesses of 'animal passion'. For many of the middle-class mothers there are nice and nasty feelings, sensible and silly behaviour. These emotional strategies are produced through a variety of practices by which the mothers regulate the emotional responses of their daughters. When daughters express violent emotions, and especially aggression towards their mothers, it is common for the mothers to respond with phrases such as 'That's not very nice' when in fact the daughter said 'I'll poke your eyes out.'
>
> (Walkerdine *et al.* 2001: 118)

Such an emphasis on 'niceness', while both important in preparing middle-class girls for social and educational success, and central to group ideas about femininity, comes at a price, and one which may be high. Not only does it involve the suppression of disagreement, it also requires a denial of difference, particularly that difference which comes from the achievement of academic excellence. Renold and Allan (2004: 7), for example, found that high-attaining girls had constantly to position themselves 'within conventional discourses of "lack", repeatedly (in interviews) denying, downplaying, hiding and silencing their successes and achievements in school'. Thus, they argue,

> being 'nice' was central to securing both approval (from others) and affiliation (to her friends) and part of this was about 'fitting in' and 'not standing out'. For 'one of the cleverest', 'most popular' and 'most attractive' girls in the class, Shamilla had to work very hard at not being different.
>
> (Renold and Allan 2004: 10)

Similarly, Brown and Gilligan (1993: 14) argue that girls have to 'give up relationship for the sake of "Relationships"', silencing their own voices and suppressing their knowledge about themselves and the world in order to fit in with their friends. The emphasis on niceness, in some ways, acts as a counter-discourse to the practices of the school: it is an open rejection of, and resistance to, the competitive nature of school life. At the same time, however, it denies academically successful girls the unalloyed enjoyment of their success, and makes it harder for them to consider themselves both feminine and clever.

The primary curriculum also presents to children an image of the world and their place in it as male or female. This allows them to construct identities as learners in alignment or in contraposition to such images. Millard (2005), for example, argues that, while girls take ideas for adventure stories from more conventional, school-based storybook sources, boys' choices range among a much wider mix of non-school media, such as videos, computer games and cartoon stories. Such choices will affect how boys and girls position themselves with regard to the school literacy curriculum, which generally treats these latter sources as illegitimate. Conversely, Letts (2001) argues that school science structures and is structured by norms of masculinity, focusing on the rationality of the mind, so that primary school science becomes a strongly masculinizing practice, in which boys can control and dominate discussions through an assertion of the priority and accuracy of their observations over those of girls.

Such domination can be hard to challenge. Jenson *et al.* (2003) report that, in a Canadian experiment in restructuring boys' and girls' access to computers, also strongly labelled as masculine, a group of girls were trained to teach other children to use particular applications. This worked well when they were passing their knowledge on to girls, but was far more problematic with boys. The latter tended to talk over them, making teaching very difficult, challenged their expertise, and would refuse help from an 'expert' girl even when they could not manage without it. The situation was in effect perceived by the boys not as an act of helping, but as one of competition with girls in a masculine arena, and they were reluctant to accept the girls' expertise.

Conclusion

Primary schooling is a central arena for the development of child communities of masculinity and femininity practice. Children use the cultures and structures of particular classrooms, schools and curriculum systems as both supports and oppositional foils for the construction of specific, localized masculinities and femininities. They do so by setting the ideas about what it is to be male or female that they have gleaned from the local community, against and alongside of examples that are presented to them through texts, curriculum forms and teachers' performances.

Such understandings of masculinities and femininities will, of necessity, vary according to local circumstances. In particular, they will be affected by the race, ethnicity and class positioning of the children involved. Both individual and group identities are formed relationally, with respect to other identities and to the circumstances, discourses and mores of the setting in which they are established. Consequently, in constructing school-based communities of masculinity and femininity practice, children will combine elements of conformity and resistance, both to the school as an institution and to other local masculinities and femininities. What is important, however, is that for some children, these constructions do not help them to succeed at school. Children who are members of strongly oppositional communities of practice will be prevented by group mores from taking a full part in the learning world of the classroom; they will be inhibited by their masculinities and femininities from engaging sufficiently also to become a member of a local learner community. Conformity can also be problematic. 'Nice', hard-working, compliant girls, while often part of the dominant community of femininity practice in primary classrooms, may at the same time be denied access to the enjoyment of their success. Those who attain it, such as Renold's (2001) 'square-girls', pay the concomitant price of membership of a more marginal community of femininity practice, and the lack of other forms of power that comes with this.

Interventions

Intervening in children's school-based communities of masculinity and femininity practice involves working at a number of levels. Because many of these are at least partially constructed in opposition to the school, it is important that the challenging of stereotypical understandings and behaviours is not carried out in such a way that it appears as another form of school knowledge against which to position oneself.

- Clearly, it is important that any explicit teaching about equity issues is taken seriously by all teachers. This is a basic underpinning principle.
- Teachers and policy-makers need to consider the impact of classroom practices on girls and boys from different backgrounds and of differing abilities, and make modifications accordingly.

It is particularly important to be aware that classroom situations which require the public performance of competence may be problematic for both boys and girls, though in different ways.

- Girls need to be supported in owning and celebrating academic success. It may be worth discussing explicitly with girls how 'being nice' can cause problems for them, as well as supporting group solidarity.
- The assumption that a competitive classroom ethos is supportive of boys' achievement needs to be questioned. While it does appear to support some groups of boys, others may be significantly disempowered and disenchanted by it.
- Teachers should attempt to model a variety of masculinities and femininities. It is important to understand that, while some masculinities in particular may allow a closer relationship between male teachers and specific groups of boys, this may occur only through the Othering and exclusion of other groups, including girls.

7 Play and children's peer groups: Constructing masculinities and femininities in outdoor spaces

The boys played boys' games on one side of the schoolhouse; the little girls played on the other side, and Mary sat with the other big girls, ladylike on the steps.

The little girls always played ring-around-a-rosy, because Nellie Oleson said to.

(Wilder 1992: 459–60)

Introduction

Child communities of practice develop most autonomously where they are least supervised by adults, and where children are free to mix widely. In this chapter I will focus on the development of communities of masculinity and femininity practice in playgrounds, both at school and in the community, considering how children use playground space, and the games they play there, collectively and relationally to construct, negotiate and consolidate their identities and performances as girls and boys. The playground is a particularly important arena for considering child communities of practice because of its status as a child-owned space. Even if adults are present, as they are in school and in some community playgrounds, they are not the focus of the action, and may (though this is not always the case) take only the limited roles of stopping fights and dealing with injuries. Karsten (2003: 471) notes that 'playgrounds are the first arenas in which girls and boys learn to negotiate their behaviour in public'. Clearly, an important aspect of this negotiation will focus on what is considered a locally acceptable performance of masculinity and femininity.

In this chapter, I will look very specifically at how masculinities and femininities are collectively constructed by children through outdoor play. I will focus particularly on how they negotiate what it is to be a boy or a girl within the spatiality of the playground. Children enact gendered power/knowledge relations in and through the ways in which they use communal spaces, and use these as part of the legitimation of certain bodily practices and mental attitudes and the exclusion of others, within particular spatial contexts.

My discussion in this chapter will draw partly on the wider literature on children's use of playground and other outdoor space and partly on my own research into tomboy identities and how they are constructed by 9–11-year-old children.[1] This is a particularly salient age group for understanding how space is used by children for the construction of identities: it is when, in developed countries, at least, they start to achieve independence from adults and older children, and begin to be allowed away from home unsupervised. It is in these relatively adult-free worlds that children's own constructions of masculinity and femininity come into play, comparatively unmediated by the restrictions and alternative constructions of the classroom and the home.

Contextualizing child communities of practice

The relative absence of adults does not mean, of course, that playgrounds are decontextualized arenas untouched by wider understandings of masculinity and femininity. The construction of child communities of masculinity and femininity practice takes place within a wider social context which has varying influences on children's behaviour, their constructions, and even their very presence in the playground. It is also important to understand that playgrounds themselves have different meanings in different social and political contexts. Karsten (2003), for example, notes that there are significant differences between school and community playgrounds. In institutional settings, she reminds us,

> when teachers and other caring adults decide so, all children have to go outside and into the playground, schoolyard or sports fields ... in residential environments, some children will visit the nearby playground, while others will not be interested, will not dare to do so or will simply be denied access.
>
> (Karsten 2003: 458)

There are thus differences in actual population between community and school playgrounds, some of which, as will become clear, are significant for the construction of masculinities and femininities.

Furthermore, how the playground is perceived by both children and adults will vary according to context. Renold (2004) notes that, for boys who are trying to construct non-hegemonic masculinities, even the supervised space of the school playground may be a place where one is frequently teased, and thus to be avoided where possible. More seriously, Bhana (2005a) points out that the school playground may be a place of ever present physical threat. She argues that, even for girls as young as 7, 'in South Africa sexual violence against schoolgirls is a daily experience. Girls are raped, sexually abused, sexually harassed and assaulted at school by male classmates and teachers' (Bhana 2005a: 169). Within these enormous variations, however, there is a consistent pattern through both the literature in the field and my own research, in which older boys dominate playground spaces (Thorne 1993; Karsten 2003; Renold 2005), using various means, while girls attempt to assert power in the face of this, through a variety of resistance strategies.

The masculinities and femininities constructed within playgrounds by local child communities of practice will, of course, be influenced by the children's perceptions of what it is to be a male or female adolescent or adult in the wider local community. This is particularly important as children get to key points in their lives, such as transfer between primary and secondary schooling, in which they consider, construct and start to take up projected identities in preparation for the move (Pratt and George 2005; Waerdahl 2005). Age hierarchies are, in any case, extremely significant in playground interactions (Scott 2002; Karsten 2003; Renold 2005); what counts as an acceptable performance of masculinity or femininity at one age will not at another, and many of the gendered playground boundaries are rendered more complex by age taboos which require boys, girls, or both, to 'grow into' or 'grow out of' particular spaces and games as they get older. As one girl in my own study regretfully said, shortly after commencing Year 6, her final year at primary school, 'apparently you're not allowed to run in year six or year seven'. Such understandings of what counts as appropriate behaviour can be quite explicit and form a significant constraint both on how children are able to construct their masculinities or femininities and on what they are able to play.

Children's collective constructions of masculinity and femininity will also be influenced by media images, both of children and adults, and by culturally marked commodities. Popular culture is mobilized by children in a variety of ways in the construction of identities. Fitzclarence and Hickey (2001) suggest that popular images of violent and determined hypermasculinities within televised sports can be mobilized to support the construction of similar masculinities within youth sports teams. Nespor (1997: 176) argues that cultural objects are 'resources for constructing identities'; some boys in his study, for example, used the collection of basketball cards as a signifier of a masculine interest in sport (though in practice some collectors knew little or nothing about basketball). Ali (2002) notes that being a 'fan' of particular singers or bands is an important marker of belonging for some girls' friendship groups. Fandom, in this context, allows the construction of particular forms of femininity around the heterosexual adoration of particular male stars. Renold (2004) reports that a preference for singers marked as more typically liked by girls acted as a signifier of alternative masculinity, both for the marginalized boys concerned and for the peer group which excluded them.

Particular forms of consumption can also be a significant marker of different forms of masculinity or femininity. Waerdahl (2005) found that children anticipating the move from primary to secondary school (at age 12 in Norway) thought a good deal about the sorts of clothing they would need to wear so as to fit in with the new peer group. Similar commodified projections into teenage futures are reported by Russell and Tyler (2005). Adler *et al.* (1992) found that designer clothing and make-up were important contributors to the popularity of US elementary school girls as early as kindergarten, and that this was also reflected in the enhanced popularity of girls from families of higher socio-economic status. In my own research, children used clothing preferences as a significant marker of different forms of femininity. Tomboy girls, in particular, were recognized by their appropriation of items of masculine-labelled clothing, such as particular designs of trainers, and among the more affluent, different designer labels were given significance in relation to various attributed femininities.

The masculinities and femininities constructed by children in their local communities of practice are also likely to be raced and classed in different ways in different contexts. Ali (2002) notes that fandom (and anti-fandom, in the case of boys) and the consequent construction of femininities and masculinities around the desire for (or hatred of) particular stars did not seem to be affected much by race in the London primary classes she studied; similarly, in my own London-based research, race did not appear to be relevant to girls' construction of their femininities. In other settings, however, it may be more significant. Karsten (2003), for example, notes that, in the Amsterdam playgrounds she studied, Turkish and Moroccan children were fewer than would have been expected given the composition of the local neighbourhoods, and girls over the age of 10–12 were rarely seen. Wider cultural mores prevalent within these ethnic groups thus prevent girls over a certain age constructing femininities within certain public spaces at all, with a concomitant effect on the femininities (and masculinities) that are likely to be negotiated there. Those who did attend, however, again formed groups that spanned social class and ethnicity.

Scott (2002), on the other hand, found that membership of predominantly white peer groups (and thus legitimate participation in particular forms of femininity) was harder for African-American children than for whites, so that gender constructions and divisions were shaped partly through an intersection with constructions and divisions around race. McGuffey and Rich (1999), in a study of a US summer camp, argue that racial and social class differences had little relevance to the power structures of boys' groups, which were based on athletic ability. Girl groups, conversely, tended to be formed on the basis of different understandings of femininity; this meant that in practice the African-American girls clustered together, due to their collective construction of a more assertive femininity than that of the majority of white girls. The girls also had a greater tendency to form class-segregated groups, as they stuck more closely to girls whom they already knew as neighbours.

Finally, it is important to understand that masculinities and femininities are constructed within children's communities of practice as almost entirely heterosexual. Although adults tend to construct childhood as a time of innocence (Epstein 1999; Renold 2005), there is, among children, a communal assumption of current and future heterosexuality. This is developed, particularly, though not exclusively by girls, through a dual culture of current and future romance, and sexual teasing of boys. 'Boyfriend' and 'girlfriend' couples can be found throughout primary school; Scott (2002) reports that some first-grade girls in the US elementary school she studied claimed to have boyfriends. Although they did not display this in the playground, other girls knew who the couples were, though it was unclear whether the boys concerned were aware of their boyfriend status. Reay (2001: 159) notes similar activities in a racially mixed group of English 7-year-olds, describing them as 'intensely active in the work of maintaining conventional heterosexual relationships through the writing of love letters, flirting and engaging in regular discussions of who was going out with who'. With older children, such relationships are more overt and mutually entered into, and can carry high status; Adler et al. (1992) note that when popular girls 'went out' with popular boys it could enhance the status of both parties, though for a girl to be associated with an unpopular boy would be tantamount to social suicide.

Renold (2005: 95), in a UK study of 10- and 11-year-old children, found that girls in particular were obsessed with heterosexual pairings in which popular children might achieve 'celebrity couple' status:

I was witnessing a daily heterosexualized social and cultural network that was all pervasive. It permeated almost every facet of school life. Beyond the girls' own emotionally charged discussions of who 'liked', 'loved' or 'fancied' who, girls' heterosexual practices included: kissing and holding hands; the setting, fixing or breaking up of relationships (usually by 'messengers' delivering secret love letters or dumping letters); sexualized playground games (such as 'blind-date'); empirically testing a range of consumer products (including a computerized 'Match-Making Diary' and a mini 'Snog Log Book' from a popular [girls'] magazine) ... Collectively these heterosexualized practices were a central and increasingly compulsory component of the ways in which the girls were 'doing girl'. Even those that resisted or rejected the sexualization of contemporary girl culture were ultimately positioned in relation to it.

In such a culture, homophobic abuse is directed at boys who do not conform to normative masculinities: masculinity is constructed as so unquestionably heterosexual that any rejection of or resistance to majority constructions brings sexuality as well as masculinity into question. Being positioned by other children as 'failed males' becomes equivalent to being 'failed heterosexuals' (Renold 2005) according to the dominant constructions of masculinity found in most playgrounds.

Constructing and consolidating masculinities and femininities through the use of playground space

Children use playground spaces in a number of ways in the construction of their own and others' identities. Identities are not constructed alone by the individual; they are developed in relation to those of others, and to spoken and unspoken group rules and norms about the sort of person one is permitted to be in a specific context. Thus, child communities of masculinity and femininity practice establish ways of 'doing boy' or 'doing girl' which privilege and embargo particular activities and spaces, according to the position an individual wishes to take up in relation to them.

These various identities and roles are related to patterns of hierarchy within intersecting child groups, so that some children have more influence than others on what identities are possible in a particular social world. Dominant individuals and groups are able to mobilize space and their own place in it to enable and gatekeep certain identities and roles. This process relates to age as well as to gender: some activities and therefore, up to a point, some identities, are only available to those of particular ages, or who are able to step outside locally accepted age boundaries. The hierarchical world of the playground (Karsten 2003) not only means that the boundaries of favoured spaces are strictly controlled by more powerful groups, but also requires that less important spaces have to be vacated as one grows older; to remain in them is an admission of subordination. This leaves some children, as we shall see, with virtually nowhere to play.

I will now look at the construction of gendered identities in play spaces in more detail, by examining it in relation to four key aspects of children's outdoor play: if they play, what they play, where they play and how they play. I will consider each in turn.

To play or not to play: immobility and the construction of girly femininities and subordinate masculinities

As girls grow older, their femininities are increasingly constructed around not playing at all, or only in the service of others. Several studies, including my own (Epstein *et al.* 2001; Kehily *et al.* 2002; Renold 2005; Paechter 2006d), suggest that, as girls move through primary school, they gradually withdraw from physical activity and spend their playtimes talking. For the most dominant and conventionally feminine girls in my own research, 'just talking' related to their status and shared identity as the oldest girls in the school: playing was considered childish, something to be left behind as one approached the move to secondary school. The importance of talking for girl groups, particularly in relation to the making and breaking of friendships (Kehily *et al.* 2002), seems to emerge around age 10 and persist into secondary school (George 2004; Renold 2005), and has an important influence on the femininities that can be constructed. In particular, it inhibits the formation of active and physically assertive femininities, by restricting girls' opportunities to experience and identify with active play.

The dominant group of 'cool girls' at Holly Bank epitomized the image of teenage schoolgirl femininity as centred around hanging around together chatting. It was clear, particularly once they had moved into Year 6,[2] that the power dynamic within this group precluded active play for its own sake. Bridget and Holly, for example, were quite clear that they only moved at all to run away from children they disliked; running around for fun was considered babyish. Instead, a passive, 'girly' femininity was constructed, focused around the negotiation of friendship and an interest in romance, 'dating' and, most of all, preserving the 'cool girls'' pre-eminence. This status was also constructed and preserved in relation to the dominant boys in the class, who were considered highly desirable and had considerable influence on what counted as acceptable behaviour. The most dominant of all, Humphrey, was clear about how a girl should behave if she wanted to be liked, stating that 'to be popular for a girl you have to be like all girly and pretty and stuff'. Such a physically passive femininity would necessarily require that a girl not take up much space in the playground.

This form of femininity was clearly enacted by the most dominant girl in the 'cool girls' group, Kelly, who was especially inactive, messing around in physical education lessons as well as opting out of playground games. Her pre-eminence within this group meant that she could require physical inactivity as the price of membership. Consequently, Chelsea and Joanna, both physically active outside school, became inactive at playtime, in the interest of preserving her coveted friendship. By contrast, during a period in which she had been ousted from the group, Chelsea led other children in a number of active and imaginative games.

As we saw in Chapter 6, several studies have noted the propensity of some girls to construct conforming, hard-working femininities around the concept of 'niceness'. Such femininities can be significantly restrictive of girls' behaviour, reinforcing constructions of femininity as unassertive (Reay 2001). In addition, 'niceness' can limit girls' play in other ways. One group of 'nice' girls at Holly Bank gave up active play because one of their number, Melissa, felt intimidated by the boys on the playground and so preferred not to encounter them by running around. Niceness would preclude leaving Melissa on her own while the others played, so they joined her in inactivity. Here, the construction of an unassertive and passive femininity combines with the culture of niceness in a self-reinforcing cycle of decreasing activity. It is noteworthy that these 'nice girl' groups do not seem to command high status in wider playground relations. Those in Reay's study were treated as contaminating by their male peers, and those in mine were referred to derisively by other children as 'the goodie-goodies'.

Subordinate masculinities can also be constructed through physical passivity and, most significantly, absence from the playground altogether. This is partly because, for those who do not take part in the dominant masculine performances discussed in the next section, the only playground space available is on the margins, with the girls and younger children. This space, because of the sex of the majority of its inhabitants, is therefore feminized, so any boy who spends time there is likely to be considered feminized in his turn, and thus subject to homophobic and other bullying. Both Renold (2004) and Bhana (2005b), studying schools in Britain and South Africa respectively, found that marginal boys tended to avoid the playground altogether, seeking out safer (though also feminized) spaces, such as the classroom or the nature garden, thereby consolidating their alternative constructions of masculinity, while avoiding the immediate consequences of taking up and performing such alternatives.

What to play: the role of playground games in the construction of masculinities and femininities

One of the most striking features of most playgrounds is the dominance of team games played almost entirely by boys. Thorne (1993: 1), for example, notes that, in school playgrounds in the USA, 'many boys, and a sprinkling of girls, spread out across large grassy fields, playing games of baseball, soccer, or football'. Similarly, Karsten (2003: 466) reports that 'the Amsterdam boys predominantly played soccer. As a consequence, they tended to play in bigger groups and control much larger spaces than the girls did'. Which games are the means for boys' spatial dominance will vary from country to country and depend at least partly on the resources available. It does seem to be clear, however, that male takeover of space is a frequent, if not ubiquitous, part of playground life, and that this is related to the construction of masculinities through sporting and related activities.

The proportion of space controlled by mainly older boys in this way can be considerable. Thorne (1993: 83) estimates that:

> boys control as much as ten times more space than girls, when one adds up the area of large playing fields (plus basketball courts and, at Oceanside, skateball courts) and compares it with the much smaller areas (for jump rope, hopscotch, foursquare, and doing tricks on the bars) where girls predominate.

In my own research, football took up approximately two-thirds of each playground, despite the two schools having significantly different amounts of space available. It is also not uncommon for marked-out pitches to be positioned centrally in the total play area, so that anyone who is not included in the game is quite literally, pushed to the margins (Epstein et al. 2001; Connolly 2003). This allows the construction of masculinities through participation in such sports to take place visibly and centrally within the local child community; such masculinities are publicly, and literally, played out.

In the British context, masculinity is overwhelmingly constructed through participation in football (Swain 2000; Epstein et al. 2001; Connolly 2003; Renold 2005). Swain (2000) argues that this is partly because boys obtain not only pleasure from the physical activity of play, but also a sense of bonding, competitiveness and comradeship. In my own research, all the dominant boys played, both in and out of school, many every playtime, and had done so since they were very young. Indeed, success at football seems to be central to attaining status within boys' peer groups, particularly when football games are highly visible to the rest of the school population (Swain 2000; Epstein *et al.* 2001; Connolly 2003).

Boys' perception of football as central to dominant masculinity means that girls – and subordinate boys (Connolly 2003) – have either to be excluded or their participation marginalized or downgraded. Anything else constitutes too serious a threat to the construction of masculinity around prowess at the local dominant sport. In many playgrounds, both within and outside school, football games are not policed at all by adults, except when fights break out, but are a free-for-all of masculine domination, in which only a girl who could fully hold her own (both socially and in terms of footballing skill) would be allowed to take part. In this context, playing football more than very occasionally marks a girl out as a tomboy, and a fairly extreme one. In circumstances where girls are supported in participation in football, on the other hand, alternative ways of distancing them from the game are employed, so that it remains available for the construction of dominant masculinities.

At Holly Bank school, for example, the close alignment of masculinity and participation in football necessitated, for the boys, the expulsion and exclusion of any form of femininity in relation to the game. In this the dominant boys were supported by the 'cool girls', who interpreted other girls' interest in football as related to a desire to attract the attention of boys, rather than to the game itself. Girls were systematically and consistently excluded from football, and therefore from much of the playground and field space. The 'cool girls' sometimes resisted such male spatial domination by walking onto the pitch and disrupting the game – something that is also reported by Renold (2005) – but they did not challenge the hegemonic understanding of football as a boys' activity by attempting to take part, thus compromising neither the boys' masculinity nor their own femininity.

At Benjamin Laurence, on the other hand, more girls participated in football, thereby challenging its strong association with dominant masculinity. This was for two reasons. First, given the relatively small size of the playground area as a whole, there was little else that girls could play if they wanted to be physically active. Second, there was a policy in the school of active promotion of football for the girls, so that they were encouraged to play and included in teams for inter-school matches. The regular presence of girls on the football pitch thus represented a challenge to the dominant construction of masculinity in this school. It was hence essential, to preserve the separation of masculinity and femininity, and to maintain male dominance, for the boys symbolically to exclude girls from football, as they could not do so physically. They did this in a number of ways. First, they almost all refused to pass to girls when they were playing, so that the girls never took a full part in the game (Swain 2000; Epstein *et al.* 2001). Second, when picking teams, girls were usually left until last and their presence complained about. Third, the spatiality of the game itself was used against girls' participation. They were always placed in defence positions, often in goal, and systematically excluded from the full take-up even of these roles: where a female defender had to do something important, such as take a goal kick, the task was taken over by a boy, while the girl watched. Fourth, girls' achievements in football were constantly belittled, with the boys repeatedly accusing them of losing matches and generally undermining their achievements. Thus the gatekeeping role of football with regard to masculinity was preserved despite girls' access to the game, with the result that, once the main force behind the inclusion of girls football had left the school, their participation dropped off rapidly.

Boys' masculinities are also constructed through fighting and aggressive play, both of which are related to violence and aggression in sports (Fitzclarence and Hickey 2001). In school, fighting is a partially staged activity containing some aspects of ritual (Nespor 1997). Swain (2003: 306) notes that 'Some of the fights I saw had an unmistakable, gladiatorial and performative nature, with crowds gathering round in a circle urging the boys on with sustained tribal chants of "fight, fight, fight" '. He argues further that, although most of the boys in his research tried to avoid fighting, it was not possible for a boy to walk away from a fight without seriously compromising his masculinity; it was 'a matter of individual honour'. Most researchers also suggest that, conversely, for a girl to fight constitutes a serious challenge to her performance of femininity, though Nespor (1997) observed the threat of violence being used by girls as an assertion of a strong, adult femininity. In my own study, girls who fought were few and far between, and were usually considered to be tomboys by their peers.

This is not to say that it is not possible for girls to develop assertive femininities through aggressive play, nor that such play is confined to boys or to predominantly masculine girls. Some aggressive but less spatially invasive games are considered to be largely the domain of girls, and support the construction of assertive and confident femininities. At Benjamin Laurence, this role was taken by foursquare, which was largely played by girls aged 8 and 9, and served as an arena in which aggressive femininities might be constructed relatively unchallenged, while also giving the girls the confidence to move onto the football pitch the following year. The game is played on a grid of four squares with four children competing at any one time and a line of others waiting to replace anyone who is 'out'. It involves the aggressive bouncing of balls into one's opponents' squares, the object being to make it impossible for them to return or to catch the ball; if they fail to do so they are called out. Successful play depends on a forceful slam-throwing style that certainly does not epitomize stereotypical femininity (Evaldson 2003). Nevertheless, the game was completely dominated by girls, who argued vociferously and aggressively with each other when called out. Boys who joined them did not take part in such disputes, but went out when called, even if they might argue long and hard about a similar decision in football. Evaldson (2003) reports similarly aggressive play in a Swedish playground. Although she found boys more likely to take part than was the case in my study, girls were similarly able to use their skills at foursquare successfully to challenge male domination.

It is unclear why this game was so strongly dominated by girls. Perhaps the relatively small area of the foursquare court, or simply the fact that it is not football, associates it with femininity; it is also possible to play it much less aggressively by banning 'slam' throws (Thorne 1993; Evaldson 2003). It is interesting to note, however, that the girls in my study who were able to argue so vociferously with each other, sometimes resorting to threats of or actual physical violence, lost much of their strong assertiveness when (as most did) they moved onto the football pitch when they grew older. It appears from this, however, that some masculinities and femininities can be enacted at a very local level, to the extent that girls and boys can inhabit strikingly different femininities and masculinities as they move from one playground area to another.

Sexual aggressiveness can also be used as a means for girls to resist boys and their constructions of femininity as passive and subordinate. Bhana (2005a) reports that the 7- and 8-year-old girls, she studied, played a sexualized game which used an overt display of their knickers, along with sexual taunting, as a way of claiming power for themselves in the face of harassment, sexual and otherwise, in the violent atmosphere of South African playgrounds:

> But, even though the girls are scared at school, they are not powerless. Girls adopt a strategy of resistance to mocking and violent boys by acting out an aggressive sexuality and investing in rudeness, lifting their dresses in concert to 'show their panties'. Their moment of power rests in 'show me the panties,' which tries to create a safer place through which their desires can be lived out.
>
> (Bhana 2005a: 168)

Similarly, games involving capturing boys and kissing them appear to be ubiquitous in playgrounds containing younger children (Thorne 1993; Epstein 1999; Scott 2002; Connolly 2003; Bhana 2005a), again affording girls the opportunity to construct and enact aggressive femininities and resist male dominance, though at the risk of adult censure.

Where to play: the interaction of gender and age-related hierarchies in playground and neighbourhood spaces

Masculinities and, especially, femininities are constructed not only *by* children through their use of space, but also *for* them as a result of restrictions on their spatial use and range. Differences between their access to playground and neighbourhood spaces and that which is allowed to boys mean that it can be difficult for girls to develop femininities that are not associated with restricted mobility and closeness to the home or the school building. Such restrictions for girls can result from parental anxieties, religious conventions or actual experience of harassment on the street. They can also be due to understandings within local child communities of masculinity or femininity practice about what is appropriate activity for boys or girls in a particular age group. This can best be understood using an example from my own research at Benjamin Laurence school, where the children held particularly strong beliefs, partly co-constructed by the school staff, about where different age groups should play.

The age hierarchies at Benjamin Laurence had a significant effect on where and what the children played. In particular, the two football pitches, Pitch One and Pitch Two, were significant high-status spaces, only open to some children. Whom they were open to changed during the fieldwork period, significantly limiting the play possibilities for girls and lower-status boys.

When the children in the fieldwork class were in Year 5, Pitch One was reserved for the Year 6 children, several girls in the study joining the boys in their class on Pitch Two on a regular basis. Some of these girls were very enthusiastic about football, which was an important aspect of their self-constructions as 'a bit tomboy'. They looked forward with eager anticipation to graduating to Pitch One the following year. The school employed a coach, Darren Thomas, to supervise both pitches several days a week. When the case study classes moved to Year 6, he decided to change this age-related hierarchy, instead designating the best players as 'Squad One' which contained no girls, giving them Pitch One as their playing area, and telling all of the other children (including those from Years 3 and 4) to play on Pitch Two. For the Year 6 footballing girls, this represented a significant demotion, particularly in relation to the boys in their class, most of whom were allowed onto Pitch One. The change in policy effectively removed many of these girls from active play and from the main spaces of the playground. Being female, for these older girls, thus became associated with an inactive spatial marginality, in which they were lumped together with the younger children as lacking in skills and therefore not deserving of a presence on a pitch that they had expected to have been theirs by right. This reconstruction of the girls' identities in relation to football, particularly as it had been set up by a member of the school staff, was extremely hard to challenge.

In this situation, a femininity associated with inactivity and spatial marginality was therefore almost being constructed for and foisted on the girls by the change in school policy. While this was resisted, such resistance seemed to take place through the adoption of a helpful, supportive femininity which resulted in being allowed to play on Pitch One as a favour, rather than a right. Gazza, a keen female footballer who was also an extremely conscientious and helpful pupil, eventually gained access to Pitch One for herself and a couple of other girls by chatting to the coach on a regular basis and running errands for him, until, after nearly a term, he allowed them to join the game. Access to football was thus only possible alongside a reconstruction of femininity in terms of helpfulness and patience, rather than a strong and skilled embodiment.

Other girls, however, may construct their femininities quite deliberately in relation to the occupation of specific and boundaried areas, as they move towards the end of primary school and the transition to teenagerhood. The 'cool girls' at Holly Bank, for example, made a deliberate choice to limit the area of the playground in which they spent their time, using this restriction as a central aspect of their construction of what was acceptable as part of 'cool' femininity. They took over a small ramp at the side of the school building, from where they surveyed the playground and intervened in the relationships between the other girls in their class, through selective offers of friendship and participation in their high-status grouping. This space, though tiny (about 8 feet by 3 feet), was ideal for their purposes. It commanded a good view of the play areas, and was surrounded, except at one end, either by the school wall or by a railing, so that there was only a small entrance space. This allowed the girls physically, as well as symbolically, to restrict admittance both to the group and to 'their' space. Other girls might be called over and invited to join, or messages to others might be dispatched from these headquarters. These girls were thus able to use the spatial arrangement of the playground in the maintenance of their position as the high-status girls in the class, controlling and commenting on the femininities of others – they were particularly focused on the issue of skirt length and the possibility that others might be 'tarts'

(Renold 2005) – while putting on a permanent and very visible display of girly femininity for their high-status male peers.

Girls' limited access to space within school is reflected in their restricted ability to function independently in the local community, echoing similar findings by Nespor (1997) in a Virginia elementary school. Karsten (2003) notes that, while children of both sexes were free to come and go in the Amsterdam community playgrounds she studied, the girls were always gone by dusk, while boys' presence continued until after dark, and older girls of Turkish and Moroccan origin were rarely there at all, except when collecting younger siblings. She also found that girls were less likely to use neighbourhood playgrounds unless they were well equipped, well maintained and clean, thus potentially limiting their access to play facilities. Such restrictions on girls' freedom of movement were found in my own research: with few exceptions, girls were limited in their access to local outdoor spaces. This had a particularly problematic effect on those girls who constructed their identities as partially tomboy. Their access to sites in which such constructions might be played out was strongly regulated: few girls were allowed out on their bicycles, to the local swimming pool, or even to walk in local streets without an adult. A pair of Turkish Muslim girls from Benjamin Laurence once challenged these restrictions by sneaking off to the local park, only to find that their male classmates were already playing there. One of them, recounting the incident, reflected sadly that 'boys get to hang out, but girls, we just stay home and have to help their mums and stuff like that'.

For these two girls, an adult Muslim femininity was something to look forward to only with reservations. They saw their lives becoming increasingly spatially and physically limited, in comparison to those of their brothers, and anticipated giving up active play at secondary school. The access that boys from the same community had to the park, and thus their greater 'ownership' of local public space, reflected their dominance in the playground and the association of masculinity with spatial control and confidence. The girls, in contrast, were increasingly expected to construct their femininities as sensible, still and studious, taking on increasing responsibilities in school and at home, while their brothers and male classmates roamed freely.

Such disparities in access to local play space are self-reinforcing. Karsten (2003) argues that people who are frequent users of a public space gain the status of 'residents', forming communities with other regular users, asserting proprietary rights to the space, dictating the rules about how it is used, and even making access difficult for others. Becoming a resident takes a considerable commitment of time; if girls are not able to do this, because of restrictions on where and when they can play, they are less likely to become residents, and may therefore have their access curtailed still further.

How you play: masculinity and taking sports seriously

Although not all sports played in school playgrounds are associated with masculinity, taking sports seriously is (Nespor 1997). Dominant boys construct their masculinities around their commitment to sports; in the UK this seems to require a reasonable level of ability, though this was not the case with the children in Nespor's US study. Associated with this, tomboy identities are constructed, both by tomboys themselves and by other children, in relation to caring about sports, and in particular about winning. In my own research this was exemplified by exhibiting distress when one's team lost, something that the majority of girls considered to be extremely silly. Two children were especially singled out in this regard: Donaldinho (a boy) and Deniz (a girl). For Donaldinho, who was repeatedly mentioned by other children as 'moaning' when his team lost, or shouting at others when their play did not come up to his exacting standards, such an attitude was an essential part of how his masculinity was constructed: he was considered to be the best footballer in his year group, and a dominant member of the 'cool boys' group in the school. The other children were generally accepting of his attitude, which, after all, was only a more extreme example of what the girls repeatedly referred to as boys 'taking it too seriously'.

For Deniz, on the other hand, 'taking it too seriously' was very clearly associated with being a tomboy. Fred and Wayne, for example, mentioned Deniz immediately when asked about possible tomboys, on the grounds that her activities and attitude were 'more like a boy':

Wayne:	Deniz's always doing runnings on Thursdays and football on the other days.
Fred:	And her attitude is more like a boy.
Sheryl:	How is her attitude more like a boy?
Fred:	It's like when her team loses.
Wayne:	She always chases people. When her team loses she's just like stunned. She starts moaning, innit.

For girls, taking sports seriously and being prepared to play aggressively (and to fight, as Deniz was) can be seen both as resistance to 'girly' femininity and as related to claims to playground and other sports space. Sheryl Clark and I have written elsewhere about many girls' reluctance to take possession of the ball or move to forward positions in both mixed and single-sex football games, suggesting that this is due to a lack of a sense of 'ownership' of the ball (Clark and Paechter 2007). Conversely, where a girl does take sports seriously this indicates a symbolic claim to (shared) ownership of the pitch, the court or the running track. By working hard at sports, and by insisting on their right to take part at the highest level, girls are claiming physical as well as metaphorical space. Those, such as Gazza and Deniz at Benjamin Laurence, who finally got to play on Pitch One, and Spirit at Holly Bank, who had challenged a teacher when she was excluded from the top cross-country running group despite coming eighth in the trials, construct their femininities partly through such participation, and, while they may not claim a tomboy identity (Spirit did, but Deniz did not) certainly stand out from many of their peers in their belief in their right to access to playground and sporting spaces.

Conclusion

I have argued in this chapter that children's communities of masculinity and femininity practice operate within a spatial context, so that masculinities and femininities become constructed partly in relation to school and neighbourhood play spaces and how they are used. What forms of identity can be taken up and maintained in any particular setting will depend, in part, on the spatial arrangements in that setting, and how they support or undermine particular power/knowledge formations.

While boys, particularly those performing hegemonically influenced versions of masculinity, dominate most outdoor play spaces, this domination is continually resisted by girls. Such resistance, however, while often aimed at challenging dominant masculinities, can also serve to consolidate particular femininities, especially in the eyes of others. At Holly Bank, for example, where the 'cool girls', despite their own relative immobility, resented the amount of space given over to football, they occasionally disrupted games by walking, arm in arm, into the middle of the pitch and just standing there, or by stealing the ball. Similarly, at Benjamin Laurence, from time to time the female footballers would get so annoyed at the boys' failure to pass them the ball that they simply stopped playing and stood in the middle of the pitch, chatting. Both these strategies reinforced the boys' and male staff's construction of the girls as not taking sports seriously and not 'really' wanting to play, and the local conception of femininity as inevitably uncompetitive was further enhanced.

Similarly, boys who resist dominant masculinities by constructing alternatives, which do not involve active outdoor play, do not thereby undermine the conceptual separation between masculinity and femininity that is typical of child communities. Renold (2004) argues that such boys still feel compelled to distance themselves from femininity, despite, or because of, their embracing of much of what is signified by it locally. Although they engaged with the ' "trying on" and embodiment of "soft" and "intimate" masculinities' (Renold 2004: 257), they did so in a context of extreme misogyny and distancing of themselves from what they perceived as feminine, thus depriving themselves of alliances with like-minded girls.

Intervening in children's collective constructions of masculinity and femininity is, clearly, a difficult and complex matter. We can, however, manipulate the spaces in which they play to make it more possible for them to take up a variety of activities in mixed and single-sex groups. This may in its turn lead to an opening up of possibilities for how identity is constructed and a greater tolerance of variety within pre-pubertal children's communities of practice. If we want children to have a wide range of possibilities concerning how they think about themselves and who they can be, we need to provide playgrounds that enable a greater variety of play activities, and which do not allow particular forms of masculinity to dominate the available space. This requires that we think much more carefully about how playground spaces are laid out, equipped and staffed, than is the case at present, and that we consider how children use these spaces, and what the implications of this use are for their self-constructions as masculine and feminine.

Interventions

Child communities are at their most independent in playground and other child-governed areas, so interventions directly into the community are unlikely to be successful. The most useful approaches are likely to involve changes to the spaces involved:

- Restrict the proportion of the space available for the local masculine-significant sport. This will involve the landscaping of other areas to avoid them being taken over.
- Encourage girls to take part in masculine-labelled sports by giving them coaching and girls-only times for play, so that they can develop their skills outside the more difficult setting of mixed games.
- Provide a wide variety of well maintained and challenging equipment to encourage both boys and girls to play actively.

- Staff playgrounds, where possible, with people trained to encourage children to try a wide variety of games.
- Do not assume that girls 'just naturally' only want to sit and talk as they grow older. Given appropriate equipment and encouragement, many will continue playing through puberty and beyond.
- In schools, encourage girls to wear suitable clothing for outdoor play. It is hardly surprising that many just want to sit and talk when they are inappropriately dressed (for example, in school uniform skirts) for running around.

Notes

1   The study, entitled 'Tomboy identities: the construction and maintenance of active girlhood' was funded by the Economic and Social Research Council (award number RES-00-22-1032) and based at Goldsmiths College, London, during 2005–6. Sheryl Clark was the research officer on this project, carrying out the fieldwork observations and interviews, and I am grateful for her support in this respect. The research was conducted at two contrasting London schools, Benjamin Laurence, a multiracial, inner-city, largely working-class school in an area of multiple deprivation, and Holly Bank, a more middle-class school in a leafy outer suburb on the edges of the countryside. Pseudonyms for schools and children have been used throughout. Those for the children are self-chosen, and so do not necessarily reflect gender or ethnicity; this will be noted where relevant.
2   This is the final year of primary school in England, entered at age 10.

8　Masculinities and femininities in secondary schools

'I have enough gunpowder in this jar to blow up this school,' said Miss Lockhart in even tones.

She stood behind her bench in her white linen coat, with both hands on a glass jar three-quarters full of a dark grey powder. The extreme hush that fell was only what she expected, for she always opened the first science lesson with these words and with the gunpowder before her, and the first science lesson was no lesson at all, but a naming of the most impressive objects in the science room. Every eye was upon the jar. Miss Lockhart lifted it and placed it carefully in a cupboard which was filled with similar jars full of different coloured crystals and powders.

'These are bunsen burners, this is a test tube, this is a pipette, that's a burette, that is a retort, a crucible . . .'

Thus she established her mysterious priesthood.

(Spark 1961: 75)

Introduction

As young people move into adolescence, school remains an important site for the construction of their masculinities and femininities. Much more than in primary school, at secondary level we see the development of small local communities of practice within which identities are constructed in relation to school, to the curriculum, and to imagined future lives (Mac an Ghaill 1994; Redman and Mac an Ghaill 1997; Reichert 2001; Kehily and Pattman 2006). While teenage subcultural communities develop outside school in relation to the media, leisure and lifestyle choices, as we will see in Chapter 9, they are subtly reconfigured within the school setting to take account of the specific spatial, bodily and mental disciplines, freedoms and constraints that are available to students, as students. In this chapter, I focus on school processes and practices and how they construct and respond to these groups, and on the school curriculum and its relationship to identity.

In considering these issues, it is important to be aware that while young people's identities are constructed within communities of practice in relation to schooling, schooling itself continues to be implicated in the construction of these communities and thereby of identity. School systems, both nationally and within particular institutions, are not passive monoliths against which identity is constructed, but instead play an active role in the construction of the communities which are found therein. They give young people messages about who they can be, what they can do and why, through the images of masculinity and femininity that they convey and purvey, and through the ways in which the capillary disciplinaries of the school act upon and are acted upon by young people as individuals and in groups.

Communities of practice, identities and schooling

Schools are particular forms of institutions, with their own kinds of power relations. These vary from school to school and between political and educational systems, but there are commonalities which operate to structure the experience of being a part of a particular school for both learners and teachers. As we saw in Chapter 6, schools overwhelmingly operate on the premise that learning requires the disciplining of the body, so that it does not intrude into the process of educating the mind (Gore 1998). This is particularly the case in secondary schooling, where the body is ignored, except within physical education, where it is treated as an entity to be trained and in which there is a conscious attempt to instil habits for particular forms of bodily future (Evans, Rich and Holroyd 2004), and in sex and relationships education, where the body and its desires are, in many ways, treated as problems (Paechter 2004). This, of course, is despite adolescence being a time during which bodies are particularly salient: they are growing and changing at what can sometimes be experienced as an alarming rate, and they may also feel slightly out of control, as hormones have their effects in ravaged skin, emotional turmoil and unpredictable menstrual cycles, as well as unbidden physical desires (Head 1997).

One manifestation of the ways in which the body in general, and sexuality in particular, are effaced from schooling is the general invisibility of students who are lesbian, gay or bisexual. This is partly because such students are threatening to dominant communities of practice of masculinity and femininity, particularly in adolescence: they disrupt the assumptions of heterosexuality that are common to young people's construction of identity. It is also, however, because lesbian, gay and bisexual bodies interfere with the overwhelming heteronormativity of schooling: a heteronormativity that is played out through sexuality and relationships education (and, in England and Wales, the legislation concerning it (Kehily 2002; Department for Education and Skills 2004)), through the invisibility of most lesbian, gay and bisexual staff (Griffin 1991; Sullivan 1993; Epstein and Johnson 1994; Sanders and Burke 1994; Sparkes 1994; Clarke 1997) and through the assumptions underlying the curriculum in general. One of the constraints on students' (and teachers') bodies in school is, therefore, that they have to perform heteronormativity (Kehily 2002): they must behave in such a way as to ensure their identification as heterosexual, rather than as transgressive, sexually Other, bodies.

This effacement of sexuality in schooling is, at the same time, only possible through the invisibility of heteronormative sexuality. The outwardly or obviously lesbian, gay or bisexual body is thus problematic to schooling because it makes sex and sexuality visible in a space where it is essential that it remains hidden. The requirements of an invisible heterosexuality therefore form a strong constraint on all bodies in school, but particularly on those for whom the performance of heterosexuality is problematic. In this way the heteronormativity of schooling restricts the masculinities and femininities that can be constructed and performed there, and supports the dominance of particular communities of masculinity and femininity practice. Those students attempting to construct masculinities and femininities around non-normative sexualities find themselves inevitably in a position of invisibility or resistance: in so doing they are causing their sexuality to intrude into a place in which it is formally absent, and refusing to allow the curriculum to construct their masculinities and femininities within a taken for granted heterosexual framework.

Where bodies intrude into school, they are seen as disruptive. The good body is self-excluding: the well-disciplined student effaces the body entirely. Evans, Rich and Holroyd (2004) argue that, for some students, the obsessive diminishing of the body that occurs in anorexia nervosa is related to overwhelming competitive pressures both to succeed acade-mically and to do well in school sports. The result, paradoxically, is that schools ignore the body even as its needs interfere with a student's well-being and performance:

> Karen: I was starved when I took my GCSEs. I wasn't eating and I wasn't drinking, I was sitting there and I couldn't concentrate. I was really dizzy.
>
> Int: Did your teachers know you were ill?
>
> Karen: Yeah, but it was important that I sat the GCSEs and got the grades.
>
> (Seventeen-year-old girl with anorexia nervosa, quoted in Evans, Rich and Holroyd 2004: 131)

For girls like Karen, the erasure of her body and its needs is an extreme form of conformity to the demands of schooling. At the same time, however, many students shape and perform their bodies in resistant and oppositional ways. In the United Kingdom, for example, the wearing of school uniform is compulsory in most secondary schools. This is a form of bodily regulation which strives to make young people as alike as possible, with the overt aim of forging a collective identity in which everyone is expected to take pride in a public performance of 'good pupil from a good school', and through which social and, in particular, financial, divisions are obscured. It also, as Shilling (1992) points out, both emphasizes the differences between male and female bodies, by specifying different sorts of clothing, and may, if skirts are compulsory for girls, restrict their freedom of movement compared to that of boys. Most students, however, find ways of altering school uniform or wearing it in such a way that this literal uniformity is resisted and undermined; policing school dress becomes, for teachers in their role as guardians of the disciplinary function of the school, a matter of daily and hourly vigilance. Epstein, in an extract from the field notes from her research in an English girls' comprehensive school, describes in detail the different ways in which the students continued to assert their individuality in resistance to the school's drive for conformity:

> Other girls (white, Afro-Caribbean and South Asian) have personalized their uniforms in a variety of ways. One, I notice, has her skirt so tight that she can barely walk and certainly has trouble when she has to sit, cross-legged, on the floor for assembly. Another presents a startling image. She is wearing the head-covering scarf usually associated with strictly orthodox Islam but is carrying a bag with a raunchily androgynous image of the current pop super-star group Take That. Several have skirts with lengths at mid-calf, the current fashion. There seem to be no (few) pleats, but several splits either at the side or the back of the skirt. Blouses, too, are individualized. Some girls have them daringly unbuttoned so that their cleavages show. Sleeves are of many different styles. Clearly there is a conscious attempt going on to individualize the uniform. This attempt is most clearly seen in the huge variety of bags which the girls carry. Clearly unregulated by uniform, these vary in size, shape and colour. Bright, shocking pinks vie with purples and greens. Some carry images of the latest pop stars. None seems to be very practical for the carrying of heavy books.
>
> (Epstein and Johnson 1998: 111)

Although for most students the adaptation of school uniform is a means of low-level but permanent resistance to the disciplines of schooling, for some it takes a more directly oppositional form. Shain (2003) describes groups of South-East Asian girls who considered the dominant school culture to be white and racist and explicitly positioned themselves against this. They did this partly through the wearing of traditional dress or, where this was not allowed, by modifying their school uniform to conform with cultural requirements (for example, by wearing trousers under their school skirts). This allowed the girls both to construct themselves as a distinct community of practice unlike the rest of the school, and to be constructed as different and deviant by others, leading to a vicious circle of racism, resistance and disaffection:

> Wearing traditional clothes certainly had a significant impact on the girls' experiences of schooling. They visibly stood out as different but chose to articulate a defence of their traditional dress. Thus dress was an important feature in asserting their identities as Asian.
>
> The girls made conscious efforts to defend their traditional outfits and to assert their preference for them. Wearing traditional clothing encouraged and enabled them to identify positively with other girls in similar attire. However, it was also one of the factors which marked them out for racist name-calling in the school because it was read against the schools' dominant white culture as a 'refusal to integrate'. Because the girls defended their traditional dress it became an important site for the contestation of school identities.
>
> (Shain 2003: 64–5)

While the students in Shain's study deliberately adopted traditional dress as part of their claim to be different from the dominant culture of their schools, for other students the situation is more fluid. Bodily comportment is often used to signify an identity within a local community of masculinity practice, and this may then be read by teachers as oppositional (Sewell 1997). Gillborn (1990), for example, describes the black British students he studied as having a particular style of walking, which was in many ways a reified marker of belonging to a particular community of practice of black masculinity (Fordham 1996). While it was sometimes adopted by students as a face-saving style when being sent out of the room as a punishment, allowing them to leave (literally) with their heads high, much of the time it was not seen by the students as a major mark of resistance, but more as one of unity with the peer group and general well-being. Gillborn (1990: 28) quotes one student's description:

> I always walk – well, it's not my usual walk sir but you know that most black people *do* walk like that [smiles] don't they? Have you ever noticed that, you know with springs in their foot and things like that. [He laughs]. I just can't help it, it's the way – it's the people I hang 'round with, and they walk like that, so you just pick it up …

Gillborn (1990: 27–9) notes, however, that whatever the intention of the student walking in this way, this performance of masculinity was consistently constructed by teachers as resistant and problematic:

> My observations suggested that the style was exclusive to Afro-Caribbean males and that it was always interpreted as in some way inappropriate by members of staff … It is impossible to say whether the teachers' negative interpretation of the style of walking was either a response to, or a catalyst for, its occasional use as a strategy of resistance. Indeed, the question is unimportant. What should be noted is that a behavioural style, rooted in the ethnicity of Afro-Caribbean pupils, was without exception interpreted by their white teachers as being inappropriate to school.

An oppositional positioning is thus constructed for the students by the school, as a consequence of bodily performances that may or may not be resistant in themselves, but which are then taken up as a form of defiance in some circumstances, reinforcing the teachers' understanding of them as problematic and resistant.

Communities of teenage masculinity and femininity practice also position themselves very explicitly in relation to schooling, taking on compliant, oppositional and other stances as part of the construction of community identities. Mac an Ghaill (1994), for example, found four clearly differentiated constructions of masculinity in the English mixed comprehensive school he studied. The 'macho lads' were a low-achieving, anti-school group, who saw school as being 'hostile authority and meaningless work demands' (Mac an Ghaill 1994: 56). In opposition to this, they constructed a masculinity focused around physical toughness, solidarity and resistance to the demands of schooling, arriving late at lessons and publicly refusing to comply with teachers' requirements. In contrast, the 'academic achievers' had a positive orientation towards schooling, an enjoyment of academic subjects, and an identity deeply informed by a strong working-class work ethic. A third group, the 'new enterprisers' could be understood as 'negotiating a new mode of school student masculinity with its values of rationality, instrumentation, forward planning and careerism' (Mac an Ghaill 1994: 63). These young men were positively orientated towards education, but specifically as a passport to good working lives later. Finally, the 'real Englishmen' were a group from a middle-class non-commercial background. They had an ambivalent relationship to schooling, refusing to affirm the legitimacy of teachers' authority and expecting to be able to negotiate curricular demands. Although they were middle-class, their identities were constructed around a 'fantasy of "proletarian authenticity"' (Mac an Ghaill 1994: 66), honesty, individuality and autonomy, and they saw themselves as both different from and culturally superior to both the other students and their teachers. In contrast to the academic achievers, they did not value schoolwork: Mac an Ghaill (1994: 67) notes that 'a key element of the students' peer group identity was a highly public display of a contradictory "effortless achievement" to each other and to outsiders', rejecting the school's dominant work ethic. Masculinities similar to this one were also observed by Power et al. (2003) among middle-class young men in highly competitive selective schools; they seem to have a way of maintaining a sense of masculinity as resistant to the demands of schooling, without jeopardizing long-term success. It is unclear, however, how strongly such a standpoint is associated only with masculinity in males: Jackson (2006) found that it was also common among teenage girls.

Similarly, Shain (2003) found four ways in which South-East Asian girls from predominantly working-class communities in England developed communities of femininity practice in relation both to racism and to the demands of schooling. The 'gang girls', as described above, constructed a strongly oppositional identity around their identities as Asian and an understanding that their schools were culturally white and endemically racist. In contrast, the 'survivors' projected a stereotypical identity as quiet, timid, hard-working South-East Asian girls, while using the opportunities school gave them for self-advancement: they were positively oriented to the curriculum as a means to a better life, 'as one way of expanding horizons for themselves, for their families, and ultimately for Asian communities' (Shain 2003: 83). The 'rebels' also prioritized academic success, but strove to blend into their predominantly white schools, wearing Western clothing in school and striving to participate in white-dominated communities of femininity practice. Finally, the 'faith girls' identified strongly with their religious communities. While this meant that their identities were constructed partially in opposition to dominant school cultures, at the same time they pursued academic success and conformed to the requirements of school, except where they conflicted with religious and cultural norms.

Such conflicts can be highly problematic for students. Fordham (1996) argues that high-achieving African-American students construct identities that are built around both society's and school's limited expectations of them and their determination to outdo these. At the same time, the young people she studied felt that in order to succeed, even in a school in which the majority of teachers were also African-American, they had to weaken and mask their African-American identities within a schooling system understood by them as structurally white. For such students, their communities of masculinity and femininity practice contain an inherent contradiction: a significant aspect of identity is collectively played down, despite being of importance to all community members. Frosh *et al.* (2002) found similar issues of identity contradiction, this time specifically around the local community of practice of masculinity, arising in relation to boys in English secondary schools. They argue that while most boys want to do well at school, boys who were popular in the peer group tended to mess around in class and not do schoolwork. For most boys, the preferred strategy was to work, but not so singlemindedly that it came to the attention of other boys; an alternative approach was to appear to do nothing in class, but keep up by studying secretly at home. Archer (2003) found that the British South-East Asian boys she studied positively valued 'being stupid' in opposition to 'serious' femininity. Some studies have found that girls, meanwhile, support these forms of masculinity by maintaining the distinction between themselves as sensible, selfless and hard-working, and boys as silly, selfish and lazy, that they constructed in primary school (Francis 2000).

Masculinities, femininities and the academic curriculum

Secondary school students, to a greater extent than younger ones, explicitly use the academic curriculum as a means for the construction of identity, by positioning themselves and their communities of masculinity and femininity practice in relation to specific subjects. Some school subjects are strongly marked as masculine or feminine, and groups of students may use this to assert or construct themselves in alignment with or in opposition to dominant notions of masculinity and femininity. How this takes place varies between subject areas, and involves both the construction of the self in relation to an image of a subject, and the construction of masculinities and femininities through the content and practices of the subject itself.

Mathematics, for example, is strongly constructed as masculine. It is understood as fundamentally rational; of the mind rather than the body; unemotional; abstract; and depersonalized – all of these have been constructed, since the Enlightenment, as masculine (Paechter 1998). Walkerdine (1988: 190) argues that mathematics, as 'Reason's Dream', 'is invested in a fantasy: a fantasy of omnipotent power over a calculable universe'. This is a strongly masculine image: as Walkerdine (1988: 199) suggests,

> The pleasure afforded [by mathematics] is ... a pleasure of control – the 'somebody else' that the mastery of mathematics makes possible is somebody who is certain, gets right answers, has closure rather than being ceaselessly caught in the web of desire. Desire is mastered. Control over and self-control become as one.

To excel at mathematics, then, is to buy into this fantasy, to identify with it. This involves taking upon oneself and claiming as part of one's identity a number of aspects of masculinity: mastery and the celebration of it; control over the world; a revelling in abstraction; and the triumph of reason over emotion. Doing mathematics, enjoying or being good at it, is therefore discursively constructed as doing masculinity (Mendick 2006). Chapman (2001) argues that learning mathematics involves learning its characteristically masculine forms of language use – precise, concise, factual and authoritative – and that, therefore, doing mathematics is about talking a particular style of masculinity, which has minimal metaphorical content and a focus on using language to assert truths. This means that to take up and maintain an identity as a mathematics student, an individual must speak and act in a particular way; she or he must perform as a member of the masculine and male-dominated community of practice of mathematics.

It is therefore unsurprising that, given the choice, girls tend to opt away from studying mathematics and related courses, particularly as they grow older and these structural features of mathematics become more pronounced (Chapman 2001). In England in 2006, for example, only 37 per cent of 16–18-year-old students taking Advanced level mathematics examinations were female. This contrasts with modern foreign languages, which are constructed, at least in English-speaking countries, predominantly as feminine, and taken by fewer boys once they stopped being compulsory. In England in 2006, 65 per cent of 16–18-year-old students taking Advanced level examinations in modern foreign languages were female (Department for Education and Skills 2006b).

The teaching of some school subjects may also operate in such a way as to dictate and limit how students construct masculinity and femininity. Martino and Meyenn (2002) note that when schools attempt to modify curricular provision to 'suit' boys or girls, they tend to reinforce, rather than challenge, gender stereotypes. Schools in the UK and Australia have recently been experimenting with single-sex classes, particularly in English, in an attempt to improve boys' performance, which is weak relative to that of girls in this subject. Because teachers bring to this situation stereotypical views about what sorts of activities boys and girls prefer (Martino *et al.* 2004), they tend to base such approaches on normative assumptions about gender. This means that not only do they provide more hands-on activities for boys and focus on stereotypical curriculum content, with 'cool, tough things' (Martino and Meyenn 2002) for boys and a greater variety for girls, they also tell students that this is what they are doing, thus actively teaching that male and female students are fundamentally different, rather than challenging normative assumptions about the nature of masculinity and femininity or working with students to understand how masculinities and femininities are constructed.

Ivinson and Murphy (2003) report that, in a school in England experimenting with some single-sex groupings for English, boys in single-sex groups were not offered the romance genre at all; it was seen by teachers as so antithetical to masculinity that they did not even consider the possibility that some boys might wish to experiment with it. Furthermore, when a few boys in the coeducational classes encountered this genre through the writing of their female peers and decided to try it, they were understood by teachers as only doing so as a way of writing pornographic material for disruptive reasons. While a high-achieving girl was permitted to hand in writing which the teacher described during feedback as 'A rather steamy Mills and Boon piece [popular romantic fiction]' (Ivinson and Murphy 2003: 104), a lower-attaining boy who attempted a similar story, but in a more action-oriented and humorous style, was not. The authors comment:

> Consequently, through his engagement with the English task, Adam came to a renewed understanding that certain practices were not legitimate for boys ... [The teacher] projected a social representation of masculinity onto the 'low ability' boys that made it essential to police and maintain the boundary for Adam by steering him away from femininely marked writing practices. She extended to Adam a hegemonic masculine identity wherein it was only possible to reconstruct Romance as pornography. Adam had no option in this setting, if he wished to succeed,

[but] to forgo his text and to fall back and comply with this extended identity. For his submitted coursework Adam produced gender appropriate texts such as a war story and a crime story.
(Ivinson and Murphy 2003: 105)

The academic curriculum can therefore be seen as highly salient to the construction of identities within school-based communities of masculinity and femininity practices. The content and form of academic aspects of schooling, and the pedagogic approaches to them, both allow students to construct themselves as masculine or feminine in relation to particular school subjects, and construct male and female students in particular ways. This happens to an even greater extent in relation to the vocational and practical curriculum, and it is to this that we shall now turn.

Masculinities, femininities, and physical, practical and vocational curricula

In considering how practical and vocational subjects support the construction of particular local communities of masculinity and femininity practice, we need to bear in mind above all that these subjects are strongly marked by social class (Skeggs 1997). 'Vocational' subjects are not vocational for all students: they lead, if they lead anywhere (and it is arguable that in some cases they do not) to skilled or semi-skilled working-class jobs. This becomes particularly clear when we consider that, in practice, academic subjects, which lead to university entrance, are themselves vocational for those students who have such aspirations (Keddie 1971). Consequently, when discussing the vocational curriculum, we need to remain aware of which social groups it is intended for, and understand its role in the construction of masculinities and femininities in these terms.

Physical and practical subjects are also marked by social class, but in different ways. The technical and domestic subjects have their histories in overt attempts, at the start of the twentieth century, to prepare working-class students, particularly girls, for gender-stereotyped forms of adult life (Dyhouse 1976, 1977, 1978; Turnbull 1987). Physical education (PE) has a history that is both gendered and classed: while boys' PE in Britain shares its history with home economics as arising from a concern for the health of working-class army recruits to fight in the Boer War (Dyhouse 1977), the female version of this subject, in both Britain and Australia, has its roots in educational gymnastics, campaigns against corsets, and concerns about the health of middle-class young women (Fletcher 1984). All three curriculum areas support the construction of highly stereotypical femininities and masculinities, often in sexually segregated contexts.

Physical education, sports, and the construction and reification of particular bodily forms as markers of community membership

Physical education and sports, particularly for boys, are most important at the extremes of social class, having a role both in the making of ruling-class men and in the construction of working-class masculinities. For each group, however, there are different forms of sport and different potential and actual rewards. Shilling (1992) argues that taking part in PE and sports can develop 'physical capital' (that is, physical abilities and dispositions that can be traded for symbolic or other commodities or for other forms of capital, such as financial, social or cultural) for individuals of all classes, but that this is differentially convertible into other forms of capital. While it is possible, he argues, for working-class people to convert physical capital into economic capital through the take-up of sporting careers, this is a highly selective and risky strategy, because of the low likelihood that an individual will succeed in a sporting career, and because participation in sports takes time from academic activities. He argues that, by contrast, for those from the middle- and upper-classes, sport is converted not into economic, but into social and cultural capital, and is used to develop particular ways of carrying and using the body, as a means of demonstrating that one belongs in specific elite social and sporting worlds. In elite schools, therefore, PE and sports are used as a way of inducting young people into particular communities of cultural and social practice that will allow them to accumulate economic capital in other ways.

Across class boundaries, however, PE both constructs male and female bodies differently and is a major site for the construction of identities within schooling, as students use the bodily practices of the subject as reified markers of masculinity or femininity. Within PE and school sports, localized versions of what it means to be a man are developed, related to physical toughness and strong, fit bodily forms (Fitzclarence and Hickey 2001). Those boys who are reluctant to participate in PE, who are not good at it, or who have physical disabilities (Martino and Pallotta-Chiarolli 2003), are thus likely to be excluded from dominant school communities of masculinity practice. These boys are considered to be so outside the community that they are treated as feminine, using terms such as 'girlie', 'sissy' or 'woman' (Salisbury and Jackson 1996), or as gay, using terms such as 'fag', 'faggot' or 'queer' (Parker 1996), which, in a context in which dominant masculinity is constructed around compulsory heterosexuality, also signifies complete exclusion.

In the communities of masculinity practice which develop in school PE and sports teams, identity becomes related to sporting competence, which demonstrates membership of the community and powerful positions within it. The competent body therefore becomes a reified marker of membership; without it one cannot become a full participant (Fitzclarence and Hickey 2001). In this way, not only do the processes of PE and school sport teach particular ways of being a man, they also induct boys into a wider community of masculinity practice in which, by virtue of their relative performance, some men are dominant and others subordinate; they reinforce the already hierarchical structures of young men's communities of practice.

Related to this is a symbolic rejection of the feminine by sporting masculinities, to the extent that it is considered impossible that a female body could display equivalent competence. Shakib and Dunbar (2002) report that male teenage basketball players were unable to accept that a girl might have beaten them in one-to-one competition because of her greater skill, instead supporting each other's excuses for losing (such as that they were never really trying), in order to save communal face. Brown and Rich (2002: 91) note that a female PE teacher who was a highly skilled footballer 'implicitly challenge[d] the stereotypical orthodoxy of males play football better than females'. The boys' reaction to this, however, was to further devalue the competence of their less skilled peers, who were teased for playing 'even worse' than a woman: 'Miss is better than you' (Brown and Rich 2002: 92).

At the same time, PE, through the practices of teachers and the ways in which the curriculum is interpreted in schools, is complicit in producing differential bodily forms for young men and women. This occurs both at the seemingly superficial level of the nature of kit to be worn, and at the level of differentiated activities and the implications these have for bodily use and development. Williams and Bedward (2002) conducted research in several English schools where girls were required to wear very short skirts for PE, even in cold weather, which made them embarrassed and reluctant to take part, thus making it less likely that they would develop strong, fit bodies. At a curricular level, activities for boys and girls may be strongly differentiated, and this affects young people's relationship to the subject. Willams and Bedward (1999) found that many girls resented the fact that they were no longer offered soccer, which many had played at primary school, and note that the curriculum offer for girls was much narrower than that for boys. While this has been alleviated somewhat in the USA by the requirement for equal resource provision mandated by Title IX (1972), problems remain even there, particularly with regard to the association of sports with masculinity and the dominance of males in coeducational classes (O'Sullivan *et al.* 2002), and there are significant differences elsewhere between what is offered to boys and what to girls.

Such differentiated activities not only emphasize physical difference but also result in boys and girls being encouraged, even required, to use their bodies in ways which emphasize particular forms of masculinity and femininity. Harris and Penney (2002), for example, note that the requirements of the English National Curriculum for PE (Department for Education and Employment 1999) that both boys and girls should gain 'knowledge and understanding of fitness and health' are being interpreted differently for boys and girls, with the avowed aim of producing different bodies:

> the use of the multigym has a different emphasis for boys and girls generally – i.e. strength development *v.* toning and muscular endurance. In cardiovascular type work, the emphasis tends to be on running activities for the boys and aerobics type work for the girls.
> (Male Head of Department, State Comprehensive School, 2000)
>
> Girls – aerobics and step aerobics. Boys – more work in multi-gym on strength and power.
> (Female Head of Department, State Comprehensive School, 2000)
> (Harris and Penney 2002: 139)

Assumptions about differences between boys' and girls' physical needs and aspirations thus lead to a differentiated curriculum, which will result in differently formed and positioned bodies. Boys will become stronger and more powerful, and girls more 'toned' – an attribute which is concerned more with appearance than with physical fitness (Paechter 2003c). It is also notable that the activities cited, aimed at 14–16-year-olds, are those characteristic of adult gym users, with men using the multigym and women going to aerobics and step classes. The school is thus complicit in supporting and legitimizing adolescents' peripheral participation in particular restricted forms of adult masculinity and femininity practices as they relate to health and fitness.

This situation is exacerbated by the ways in which many dominant teenage femininities have elements that are constructed around a rejection of the physical, powerful use of one's body and, in particular, of organized school PE. This represents a localized view (or a constellation of localized views) of what it means to be a woman. Cockburn (1999) notes that girls' teenage magazines not only put enormous emphasis on femininity and heterosexual desirability, but also position participation in sports as being in contrast to this. Images of stereotypical femininity are set against those of sport, girls' bodies are overwhelmingly presented as a problematic source of embarrassment, rather than pleasure, in PE scenarios, and girls' involvement in physical activity is given little or no value. PE thus has an important role in the development of the exaggerated femininity characteristic of many adolescent communities of practice, because the practices of these communities are often constructed directly through the rejection of PE and sports and of strong, fit, bodily forms, even despite the already feminized bodily uses characteristic of secondary school PE.

Girls expect to participate in adolescent communities of femininity practice constructed in this way, even before they reach secondary school. In my own research carried out with Sheryl Clark on tomboy identities, 10- and 11-year-old girls anticipating their transfer to secondary school generally thought that they would give up most of their physical activity, even though it was something they valued: they seemed to consider it as an inevitable part of taking on an older, more serious, femininity. As one girl regretfully remarked:

Nilay: I think that I am going to change because I'm not gonna play football anymore and I'm not gonna want to play, it's gonna be like I've just gotten old and I've got to more concentrate on my work.

It seems that as girls move nearer to participation in local communities of practice of adult femininity, they realign their understandings of themselves so that they consider their bodies to be physical in other, more stereotypically feminine, ways. At the same time, a growing awareness of their bodies makes girls more likely to reject PE because of the elements of display involved, especially in gymnastics, in mixed groups, or when they are forced to wear very skimpy clothing (Williams and Bedward 1999, 2002). As they start to take part in the communities of practice of femininity that are found in secondary schools, girls are expected to reject the possibility of themselves as being physically embodied as strong and fit. They embrace a softer, more physically helpless identity which is more closely aligned with wider notions of femininity in society and the media.

Practical and vocational curricula: Segregating working-class students

Vocational and practical subjects are also strongly labelled as masculine or feminine, both by the students themselves and by the practices of schools and colleges. In most countries, practical subjects have their origins in a working-class, gender-segregated curriculum that taught various configurations of home economics to girls and resistant material and workshop crafts to boys, though it is now usual to have all varieties offered to both sexes, and, in some cases, an officially gender-neutral curriculum (Paechter 2000). The ways in which these subjects are perceived, however, and gendered patterns of take-up in particular, mean that they are still implicated in the construction of socially classed masculinities and femininities in complex ways.

In England and Wales in the early 1990s, for example, there were strong, government-led attempts to develop a gender-neutral subject, design and technology, from the former subject areas of home economics (food and textiles) and craft, design and technology, originally designed for females and males, respectively. It was not long, however, before this was changed to provide a core of resistant materials teaching for 14–16-year-olds, with a choice of additional food, textiles, or resistant materials technology (Paechter 2000). These choices are made on strongly gendered lines. In England in 2006, for example, boys made up 94 per cent of 16-year-olds taking the electronic products option, 83 per cent of those taking resistant materials, and 93 per cent of those opting for systems and control, but only 30 per cent of those taking food technology and 3 per cent of those taking textiles technology (Department for Education and Skills 2006a). This means that, from age 14 onwards, these classes are predominantly single-sex; the curriculum is segregated in practice, if not in theory. There is some evidence that such segregation leads teachers to construct the relation-ship between the minority group and the curriculum differently from the way it is constructed for the majority. Attar (1990), for example, argues that boys taking home economics classes are expected to approach the subject much less seriously and with a greater sense of fun than are girls. It is also the case, however, that these classrooms can be experienced by both girls and boys as strongly gendered spaces, even when the numbers of each are equal: Dixon (1997) describes an incident in a resistant materials workshop in which one boy uses the woodwork tools to sexually harass the girls by pretending a mallet is an erect penis. She notes that:

> Like other boys in the group, he feels comfortable in the workshop and regularly enacts this through appropriation of equipment and resources. He and others frequently store tools or materials in their pockets or trouser waistbands, or sit on them to avoid others using them, exhibiting a degree of comfort and safety in this environment. They have come to regard it as in some way 'their space'. No girl in this group acts in this way.
>
> (Dixon 1997: 94)

The gender differentiation of the curriculum is particularly strong in vocational subjects, which are offered to young people from age 14 in many countries (Gaskell 1995; Münch 1995; Equal Opportunities Commission 1999; Cho 2000; National Women's Law Center 2002; Pae and Lakes 2004). Mjelde (2004) notes that even in the Nordic countries, where gender equality is so well established that it is seen as natural and inevitable, vocational courses remain strongly gender-segregated, with girls studying shorter courses in home economics, health and social services, aesthetic and handicraft subjects, and boys manual, electrical and building trades, in which apprenticeship contracts and craft certificates are available, thus leading to more lucrative jobs. Kraus and Carter (2004) argue that since unification, gender divisions in vocational choices in Germany have been exacerbated: young women in the East have moved from more or less gender-neutral career preferences towards aspirations that reflect more stereotypical femininities. In the USA, gender segregation in vocational courses at high school level is widespread and pervasive. For example, in a study of students in vocational programmes in 13 states, the National Women's Law Center (2002: 4) found that:

> Female students make up 96% of the students enrolled in Cosmetology, 87% of the students enrolled in Child Care courses, and 86% of the students enrolled in courses that prepare them to be Health Assistants in every region in the country. Male students, on the other hand, comprise 94% of the student body in training programs for plumbers and electricians, 93% of the students studying to be welders or carpenters, and 92% of those studying automotive technologies.

Similar levels of gender segregation are also to be found in vocational courses in the UK (Equal Opportunities Commission 1999, 2001).

Two features of this situation are highly salient in the construction of masculinities and femininities in school. The first is that this construction will take place differently in situations which are completely, or almost completely, single-sex. The formation of particular kinds of communities of masculinity and femininity practice that are centred around the group within a vocational course is more likely when all or most of a student's time is spent with this group, as is the case in vocational schools. Lakes (2004), for example, argues that in an automotive class he studied, a white working-class masculinity was constructed in which white maleness was embodied as a marker of moral and cultural superiority in which white women were seen as chattels who had to be prevented from interracial dating. The second is that, in some cases, the vocational subjects themselves act to construct masculinities and femininities in particular ways. Skeggs (1997) notes, for example, that courses focused on caring roles are strongly under-pinned by an assumption of heterosexuality, to the extent that women are directly educated to be heterosexual, through assumptions about correct forms of caring and, in the cases she studied, through the discussion of marriage as a curriculum topic. Pae and Lakes (2004) describe female students in Korean commercial high schools as being trained to comport themselves in stereotypically feminine ways, and to enhance their physical attractiveness. These are specifically vocational attributes in this context (Korean businessmen often require attractive-ness in their female employees, and may even spell out height and weight preferences in job advertisements), but they also construct the students in particular ways. A young woman who is not prepared to conform to these prescriptions is not just unlikely to get a job in the commercial sector: she is also a non-compliant student.

It is also highly significant that the take-up of vocational options is strongly influenced by social class. Vocational schools and courses are predominantly inhabited by working-class young people (Kraus and Carter 2004), while middle-class students are more likely to remain within academic, university-track curriculum provision. This means that there is a clear difference in what is offered, not just in curricular terms, but in terms of the settings in which masculinities and femininities are constructed, for young people of middle-class and working-class origin, after the age of about 14. Middle-class students will continue to study in mixed classes, with a curriculum which, while rooted in Enlightenment forms of masculinity, supports and represses particular forms of masculinity and femininity, but which, in particular, gives emphasis to middle-class forms of thinking, working and being. Working-class students will be more likely to spend the final years of their education in groups of predominantly one sex, learning and constructing working-class masculinities and femininities that prepare them for strongly classed and gendered roles in society and the job market.

Conclusion

Despite the increasing influence of the wider social world, in the secondary years masculinities and femininities remain strongly influenced by the processes and practices of schooling. Schools act in a number of ways to influence how communities of masculinity and femininity practice can develop and what forms they can take. They have a powerful role in the formation of understandings of the body, both through the formal curriculum of PE, and via their work in the effacement and sidelining of young people's bodies, which serves to both produce a heterosexual normativity and to support particular understandings of raced, classed and gendered bodies. Masculine and feminine bodily practices are also produced in resistance to schooling: while the school endeavours to keep the body out, students work hard to bring it back in and, in doing so, construct themselves as male or female in particular ways.

As an institution whose overt purpose is to provide opportunities for learning, the school also gives students enormous opportunities to construct their masculinities and femininities in conformity or opposition to its requirements. School-based communities of masculinity practice are, for the most part, focused around an overt opposition to schoolwork, so that those who do it are either marginalized (if their conformity is obvious) or have to study in secret. Conformity to the work demands of schooling, on the other hand, is much more acceptable in communities of femininity practice (Francis 2000; Frosh *et al.* 2002), though conspicuous effort is still likely to prevent an individual from reaching high levels of personal popularity (Jackson 2006).

Furthermore, the school curriculum itself acts as an important force in the construction of local communities of masculinity and femininity practice. Because some curriculum subjects are strongly labelled as masculine or feminine, students are forced to take up positions in relation to these, and this positioning in itself influences how their masculinities and femininities are constructed. Strongly masculine-labelled subjects are, in particular, problematic for girls who, in taking them up, have to acknowledge and accept aspects of their own masculinity which may be less than acceptable to their peer communities and leave them open to the risk of marginalization (Mendick 2006). This stereotyping of subjects and subject content as masculine or feminine restricts the possibilities open to both boys and girls and can severely limit their future possibilities. This is particularly problematic in the case of vocational qualifications, where young women overwhelmingly opt for pathways that lead to poorly paid jobs with little possibility for advancement or the development of their skills, in contrast to young men, who tend to favour those courses leading to recognized trade qualifications with the potential for self-employment and good rates of pay (Equal Opportunities Commission 2002).

Interventions

It is important to understand here that when I am discussing interventions in how communities of masculinity and femininity practice are constructed in relation to secondary schooling, I am not following the recent trend in some countries towards providing curricula and learning activities that are considered to be 'more suitable' for boys and girls. There is considerable evidence that these are more likely to reinforce stereotypical, heteronormative ideas about masculinity and femininity and to further marginalize those students who do not conform to these (Martino and Meyenn 2002; Ivinson and Murphy 2003; Martino *et al.* 2004). My intention, instead, is to consider how we can intervene to support more flexible constructions of masculinity and femininity, and to resist the dominance of particular understandings of curriculum and curriculum forms.

- The exclusion of the body both from education and from educational research (Paechter 2006c) is a serious problem. We need to find ways in which we can acknowledge, and give more freedom to, students' bodies outside of the practical subjects and sex education. There is little evidence that the strong bodily policing that occurs in school is really necessary.
- Teachers should be given much more support in understanding in detail the construction of masculinities and femininities in schools. This will help them to construct interventions that do not reinforce stereotypes.
- It is essential to support lesbian, gay and bisexual students and teachers in school, and challenge the heteronormative assumptions that underlie both school bodily practices and academic and practical curricula. It may be possible to do this through discussion of the varieties of bodily performance and their implications.
- Those counselling students about career and subject option choices need to take a strongly proactive approach to ensuring that young people are fully aware of the implications of their choices for their future lives. More work needs to be done to support those who make non-stereotypical choices, particularly if they then find themselves in a small minority in the classroom.
- Teachers should make themselves more aware of when their assumptions about gender differences, or their taken for granted ways of working in classrooms, construct masculinities and femininities in particular ways for particular groups of students. Some of this happens very much at the micro level and can be addressed through peer observation and discussion.

9 Being and becoming: Learning masculinities and femininities in teenage communities

Toni and I were strolling along Oxford Street, trying to look like *flâneurs*. This wasn't as easy as it might sound. For a start, you usually needed a *quai* or, at the very least, a *boulevard*; and, however much we might be able to imitate the aimlessness of the *flâneurie* itself, we always felt that we hadn't quite mastered what happened at the end of each stroll. In Paris, you would be leaving behind some rumpled couch in a *chambre particulière;* over here, we had just left behind Tottenham Court Road Underground station and were heading for Bond Street.

(Barnes 1980: 17)

Moving towards adulthood: Communities of being and becoming

As they become aware that they are replacing peer for family society, adolescents develop a new sense of age-group member-ship. They are no longer members of an age group imposed upon them by the age-graded structure of the family, but of an age group that they have chosen as an alternative to the family. With the development of a sense of membership in an age group separate from, and opposed to, adult, they acquire responsibility for this age group and develop a stake in its structure and norms. As the alternative to the family as a basis for identity, adolescent society must appear to them worthy and reliable. Thus, the means of acquiring independence becomes a communal issue within the age group, and adolescents develop a sense of responsibility not only for their own behaviour but for that of their peers.

(Eckert 1989: 74)

Communities of practice of masculinity and femininity in adolescence, in common with other adolescent communities of practice, are positioned ambivalently between being and becoming. On the one hand, as adulthood approaches, the question 'what sort of person do I want to be?' looms ever larger, with its accompanying anxieties, fears, and thoughts of the future (Head 1997). On the other, adult society does not always appear to be something to aspire to (Cullen 2005): teenagers are not always in a hurry to take on adult roles and may explicitly want to enjoy their relative lack of responsibility while they can (Gordon *et al.* 2005). Consequently, while adolescent communities of masculinity and femininity practice are deeply concerned with trying out ways of being adults, they are also frequently constructed in opposition to adulthood, refusing adult norms and being explicitly teenage groups of which adults may not be legitimate members. They are very much groups of transition, communities in which aspects of adulthood may be tried on and played with, considered and accepted or rejected. Furthermore, individuals are likely to move through a series of adolescent communities on the route from childhood to adulthood: Griffiths (1995) notes that the composition of friendship groups among teenage girls is at least partially dependent on how much they have moved into adolescence, with those at similar stages sticking together. At the same time, she argues, multiple participation in teenage friendship communities, through school, orchestra, clubs, the local area, and so on, facilitates the transition from childhood into and through adolescence by permitting young people to take on different roles in different contexts.

In these communities, aspects of adulthood are tried on and experimented with, but may not be taken up as long-term projects; they can instead be thought of as tentative sallies into the serious world of adult life. Williams (2002: 30), for example, says of the 13-year-old girls in her study that they 'considered, talked and laughed about dieting and dating and then postponed enacting such activities for a more grown-up time'. Similarly, Cullen (2005: 10) notes that older British teenagers move from the adult world of the pub, where they have gathered in the winter evenings, back into parks as soon as the weather allows it, arguing that

> some young women were reluctant to take the step from outdoor ... space, such as the park, to pubs and house parties, due to the responsibilities of adulthood and an acknowledgement of the differing set of social codes involved in socializing in these adult spaces.

These transitions may also focus around reified objects with which particular communities of masculinity or femininity practice are associated. Kehily (2002) notes, for example, that the 14- and 15-year-old girls she studied felt that magazines aimed at slightly older young women were so sexually explicit that a girl's reputation might be compromised by reading them. This is unsurprising, given McRobbie's (1996) finding that the journalists writing for these see their readers as an extension of their own friendship group. The younger women can be seen to be positioning their own community practices of femininity against those of young adults by regarding the mores of the latter as going too far.

Although the communities of masculinity and femininity practice that are constructed by young people are in many ways oppositional (and perceived by their members as oppositional) to those of local adults, at the same time they are positioned within and structured by local adult norms and values. This can happen in a number of ways. First, communities of becoming are strongly influenced by local under-standings of what it is possible to be. In constructing a community that has as one of its central features that it is moving, however reluctantly, towards adulthood, members are limited by the horizons in front of them, by the expectations of the local adult communities (Willis 1977; Skeggs 1997). These limitations differ according to social class, race and location. Williams (2002: 42), for example, explains how girls' femininities are restricted by local adult communities of femininity practice, even in a relatively privileged, university-focused town:

> The Greenville girls began to build an idea of womanhood that is characteristic of the local gender regime. Women (as an ideal type) look good, make themselves desirable to men, and generally choose compliance. But women also are assertive, they can play sports, demand equal access and resources (even if they do not always get it), and they value competition. They understand that competition with men is how women are often judged, and they begin to practice those contests.

Within these overall parameters, the one thing that is most obvious about adolescent communities of practice is the degree of fragmentation between them. While child communities may be relatively large and loosely focused around a school class or those who frequent a playground or live in a neighbourhood, teenage communities are much smaller and more numerous, as well as being strongly exclusive. Eckert (1989) suggests that these divisions arise around the time of transition between primary and secondary schooling, and that this may be associated with the rite of passage between childhood and preparation for adulthood that this constitutes, although she also argues that they are a development of earlier subdivisions within a more fluid peer community. In adolescence, however, these become solidified around different ways of understanding the self and identity. By associating with one teenage subgroup or another, a young man or woman is asserting that they are a particular kind of person, and, both by implication and by explicit opposition, not another kind.

It is within these relationally constructed subcultural groups that adolescent communities of masculinity and femininity practice are themselves constructed. An individual is, therefore, not just a teenage boy or girl, but a skater, a jock, a grunger, a goth, a burnout, a townie, a grebo or whatever. The simple divisions between, for example, tomboys and girly-girls make way for complex elaborations of difference, which have continually to be worked on and refined. Kehily and Pattman (2006: 39) note, for example, that 'the construction of middle-class identities for students involves constant struggle and unrelenting, reiterative differentiation from others', while Eckert (1989: 49) points out that this oppositional definition will seize upon any possible way of differentiating between the groups involved:

> Unstructured differences that have developed through elemen-
> tary school are imbued with significance as they are thrown into
> opposition, and the opposition itself gains hegemony as it
> absorbs more and more aspects of everyday life. In an effort to
> differentiate themselves, the two categories progressively sepa-
> rate their worlds, developing opposing territories, appearances,
> demeanors, and activities.

The complexities of these differentiations mean that group members, particularly those belonging to communities which are able to mobilize significant social power, have continually to police their own and others' behaviour to ensure that it is in conformity with the current and repeatedly renegotiated norms of the group. This requires a constant mutually panoptic gaze, so that everyone is always under the scrutiny of everyone else, and is at the same time self-policing. Indeed, this endless re-examination of the self is necessary not just because one is always in danger of having one's legitimate membership called into question, but also because it is through group membership that one defines who one is and is becoming.

In consequence, it is through these adolescent communities that young people can work out with greater precision the sort of people they want to be: their fine differentiations support the thinking through of personal positions. At the same time, this multiplication of difference and close focus on the norms of the group can be enormously constricting to individuals: to become a central participant, and thus to be able to change the rules, one has first to demonstrate that one is a fully functioning and conforming member. This may be particularly important if one is a member of a socially powerful or, on the other hand, a strongly oppositional community. Different groups, and different individuals within groups, have varying access to social power, so that in and between these communities of masculinity and femininity practice there are large discrepancies in ability to mobilize power relations to individual and group advantage. Those who are able to do so are labelled as 'popular', though this may be more to do with high social status (in particular, being a central participant in a powerful community of practice) rather than being well thought of by others (Duncan 2004; Aapola *et al.* 2005). Thus in any local community of teenagers there is likely to be a 'popular crowd': a group whose practices are such (and this will vary according to the wider social situation) that they are able to dominate others and resist challenges to their hegemony. Other groups may then define themselves in opposition to this group (Eckert 1989), and are thus likely to be regarded as outsiders, though they may wear this status as a badge of pride, seeing themselves as self-consciously different from the mainstream. The 'lads' in Willis's (1977) classic study of working-class teenage masculinities, for example, constructed themselves in opposition to the 'ear 'oles' whose conformist behaviour they despised. In such a situation, individuals may gain stronger positions within the oppositional group as a result of their closer identification with oppositionality. Thus, social power becomes bound up not only with the ways in which communities align themselves with other aspects of the locality (for example, those who conform more closely to locally powerful adult communities of practice may gain more access to resources, because they will appear trustworthy to adults (Eckert 1989)) but also with the ways in which their community-based identities are played out within that community. In this way, the storying of identity through the community of practice, the ways in which individuals tell themselves to themselves, becomes bound up with the practices of the community and the power relations within and between communities.

Telling one's identity: Performing the self to the self and others

A major aspect of adolescence is the process of working out what sort of person one is, and is not. This can involve the performance of and experimentation with possible selves, as part of the 'trying on' of identity. It also requires strong differentiation between these different ways of being, so that one can be clear about the variations between and implications of these possible identities. There is thus a tendency for teenagers to divide themselves up into relatively small communities of practice, developing boundaries between themselves and outsiders through an Othering process. Local masculinities and femininities are developed within these, so that adolescent communities of masculinity and femininity practice are subsets of specific, clearly differentiated communities. This means that, for example, being a skater *girl* involves not just identification with the skater community, but membership of the community of femininity practice within that, which will be different from the corresponding skater community of masculinity practice (Kelly, Pomerantz and Currie 2005).

Gulbrandsen (2003: 129) reports that the Norwegian girls she studied tended to emphasize and justify the choices they made by saying that 'I am a person of this kind'. This, she argues, is a way of giving continuity to the process of self-construction, presenting oneself as a coherent identity in which who one is fundamentally affects how one behaves. She also notes that girls use talking within the group to negotiate ways of being themselves as a girl amongst girls, so that the sort of girl one can be (reflected in the things it is acceptable to do) is constantly discussed, modified and refined. This labelling of the self can be centrally important: Archer (2003) reports that the young British men of South-East Asian origin, she studied, wanted explicitly to label themselves not just as Muslim, but as black, as part of a claiming of a strong, political identity in the face of perceived oppression. Blackness, in this case, was associated with powerful, resistant masculinities that were positioned starkly in contrast to the popular image of weak and passive South-East Asian masculinity. It also contrasted with the self-image of local Muslim girls, who identified themselves as British Muslims. Such identifications can also be with local territory: in another study, Archer and Yamashita (2003) found that an ethnically mixed group of young men labelled themselves very explicitly as 'Harkton boys'. This identity not only tied them closely to their locality but also cut across racial and ethnic boundaries, uniting them through common local roots and experiences.

Such explicit labelling of oneself as being a member of a particular community of masculinity or femininity practice enacts and demonstrates a commitment to that community. This may be very positive and reinforcing of an individual's sense of membership and participation. Fordham (1996) writes of the larger black community in the United States as having a sense of fictive kinship, whereby loyalties to other black people are prioritized over other possible connections. Way (2004) notes that the African-American and Latino boys she studied had strong expectations of friendship in terms of loyalty, brotherhood and intimacy. Membership of a close friendship group involved high levels of trust, including the sharing of money and an expectation that friends would keep one another from harm. This was reflected in the way in which the young men spoke about each other, repeatedly referring to their closest and most loyal friends as 'brothers', giving them the status of family members.

For Archer's (2003) young South-East Asian men, naming themselves explicitly as Muslim was part of associating themselves with a global Muslim brotherhood, providing them with a source of solidarity and status. This self-labelling acted as a claim to legitimate participation in the strongly masculine-marked practice of defence of the honour of Islam as a religion, in particular through the policing of the behaviour of their sisters and female peers. Such masculinities were very much enacted within a British urban context, however, and appear to have had largely symbolic force: most of the boys did not take part in key practices of the religion they so strongly identified with and wished to defend. They did permit, however, the reinforcement of masculine privilege within a patriarchal culture, allowing the boys to argue for the perpetuation of 'tradition' in the face of changing gender relations within wider society.

While naming oneself in a particular way acts as a claim to be a member of a particular community of masculinity or femininity practice, membership nevertheless has to be earned. Eckert (1989: 79) reports that the largely working-class 'burnout' group in her study were inducted into group behaviours and attitudes in the summer preceding their entry into junior high school, as they were gradually allowed to take part in the adolescent peer community in their home locality:

> As they approached junior high school, many sixth graders in the 'Burnout' neighborhoods gained access to evening group activities with the older members of their networks. Most important of these activities for the development of category consciousness were evening gatherings during good weather in neighborhood parks. During these gatherings, the sixth graders were introduced to smoking, marijuana, heterosexual relations, and discussions of adolescent social structure and adolescent problems.

New members were thus initiated into the practices of the group, even before entry into the arena where this particular identification was especially salient in its oppositional positioning and self-differentiation from the alternative community of 'jocks': the world of the junior high school. Once there, these behaviours and identities were further elaborated as part of the new members' apprenticeship to and initiation into the mores of the group.

Some communities of practice explicitly teach new members how to construct narratives of the self within the community and to others. This has been described elsewhere in relation to members of Alcoholics Anonymous groups (Lave and Wenger 1991), and support groups for transsexuals and transvestites (Mason-Schrock 1996). In these cases, there is a process by which elements of new participants' personal stories are supported, developed and confirmed by central members when they conform to the community's co-constructed identities, and ignored and sidelined when they do not. In this way, new members learn to produce a story of the self according to the mutual understandings of the community of practice, so that a shared pattern of personal history is developed and supported. Similarly, some adolescent communities of masculinity and femininity practice support and develop particular ways of telling the self, both within the community and to a wider audience. Davies (2005) notes that online communities of teenage Wiccans use their websites and message boards both to emphasize the key features of their religion and to police the mores of a community which has, among other things, a strong identity associated with persecution. Analysing websites constructed by teenage girls describing themselves as Wiccan, she notes that pictures of altars and descriptions of how to set them up are common, allowing new members to see what they need to do to participate, and there is much material on the sites arguing for the right to worship and describing the martyrdom of previous witches. She argues that 'many Wiccans see it as their duty to teach others about the right way of doing things' (Davies 2005: 13). Consequently, the Wiccan principle that no harm should be done to others is repeated across sites, and such warnings that 'the spell will become less powerful if you tell people about it' (Davies 2005: 13) are frequently found on message boards. Through these and other features, central members of the online community of teenage witches support and guide the development of Wiccan femininities within this geographically dispersed but in other senses local community of femininity practice.

This guiding of new participants' stories of themselves is related to and develops into collective storytelling within the local community of masculinity or femininity practice. Nayak and Kehily (2001) describe how British teenage boys use the collective telling of humorous stories about each other to construct strong masculinities of resistance to school constraints. In these stories, which were collectively repeated over time, the masculinity of some boys was confirmed, while that of others was called into question as sexually incompetent or gay. The telling and retelling of community legends thus draws and reinforces the boundaries of practice of the community, while confirming particular individuals in their position as central members. Haavind (2003) notes that similar stories about 'making hell' were repeatedly recounted by Norwegian boys performing a strongly resistant masculinity, supporting their transformation from childhood into adolescence. Similarly, Cullen (2005) argues that young women use stories of risky behaviour, particularly in relation to alcohol, both to foster group cohesion and to reinforce the boundaries between acceptable and unacceptable behaviour. This involves a considerable degree of mutual policing. She describes one incident where a girl recounted drunkenly accepting a bottle of cider from an older male stranger at the river bank. She argues that in telling such stories and thereby performing and storying their identities,

> young women had to tread a tightrope of fulfilling the group norms in this peer group. These codes were not explicit, but ... girls would gradually learn how to tell the story and become a greater part of the group. The more dominant girls in the group, who would play to the crowd, most often told the drinking stories. The other people in the group, including the youth workers, would listen, laugh, and give support to the storyteller. The 14 year old in her cider story momentarily misread the social codes, and instead of getting support from the group for her daring, found herself getting impromptu advice about date rape drugs from young women and youth workers alike, with narratives of sexual violence and fear of date rape acting as a cohesive agent in uniting the young women in their shared identity as women and as potential victims.
>
> (Cullen 2005: 21)

Canaan (1986) further demonstrates how the collective telling of stories about the sexual exploits of other young women consolidates the majority group's construction of acceptable sexuality and sexual practices in ways that mutually police and limit their behaviour, constructing as acceptable a limited range of sexual practices through the Othering, as 'sluts', of those who go beyond these.

Kehily (2002) argues that problem pages in teenage magazines also provide a collective approach to storytelling which demarcates acceptable behaviour within a particular community of femininity practice. She notes that young women reading problem pages focus on the problem, only reading the advice given if they feel that the problem applies to them. Through the communal reading of problem pages, girls learn a particular way of telling their emotional lives, 'giving experiences a vocabulary within the language of the felt' (Kehily 2002: 114), within local communities of femininity practice. Because young women collectively negotiate how to respond to the problems, agreeing between them what are appropriate responses to the issues being raised, such group readings function to construct and reinforce boundaries between those in the group and outsiders whose behaviours or concerns are collectively deemed unacceptable or ludicrous:

> My discussions with young men and women indicate that young people collectively negotiate their responses to problem page features within the context of friendship groups. Here friends act as mediators and regulators of 'problems', determining whether they should be dismissed, humoured, taken seriously or discussed further.
>
> (Kehily 2002: 114)

Only some problems count, and if yours do not, then you may no longer be able to consider yourself as a full member of the group. This is particularly the case if your problems indicate a sexual licentiousness beyond the strongly policed norms for group behaviour.

Through all these ways in which identity is constructed and performed, two themes run through the literature. The first is the association of femininity and caring. Skeggs (1997) suggests that caring is more productive of femininity than investment in appearance; both are fundamental to female respectability. Brown and Gilligan (1993), in a study of middle-class American girls, suggest that as teenagers they feel compelled to prioritize their interpersonal relationships over telling the truth about the world as they see it, suggesting that this strong emphasis on mutuality and caring transcends class boundaries. Aapola, Gonick and Harris (2005) argue that girls' friendships are organized around a set of ethical rules that emphasize reliability, reciprocity, commitment, confidentiality, trust and sharing, and this is reflected in Hey's (1997) suggestion that 'being nice' is central to the construction of many dominant femininities well into adolescence. It is unclear to what extent this emphasis on niceness is raced and classed. Aapola, Gonick and Harris argue that it is a specifically middle-class preoccupation that is related to the control of emotions, and that working-class girls are less afraid to express differences and resentments. George (2006) also argues that black British girls may set more store by truth-telling than by the caring, compliant image that is part of the requirement of niceness. Duncan (2004) suggests that, while niceness is important to adolescent girls, it does not confer social power: the officially popular girls in her study were not 'nice', but brash, aggressive, involved in rumours and fights, and unafraid to ostracize or physically abuse girls who challenged their position. It may therefore be that caring and being nice are important resources for members of relatively subordinate communities of femininity practice. A caring femininity is one which is in many ways unimpeachable (Skeggs 1997), and stands in contrast to the cultural unacceptability of female displays of aggression (Aapola, Gonick and Harris 2005). By positioning themselves as thoughtful and caring, members of these groups can claim a moral superiority over those by whom they are intimidated, thus permitting themselves to feel the power of their goodness and respectability, even if that power is not available for mobilization.

A second theme to be found in the literature on adolescent masculinities and femininities is the association of masculinity and danger. Mills (2001) argues that the extent to which a young man can demonstrate risky behaviour to his peers is important to his position in local hierarchies. Consequently, those who are from marginalized backgrounds take the greatest risks, whether these be physical, emotional or social. Cunningham and Meunier (2004) note that the young, generally impoverished African-American boys in their study tended to take bravado attitudes to problems, refusing to admit any emotional vulnerability. Nayak and Kehily (2001) report that teenage boys test this supposed invulnerability by engaging in ritualistic 'cussing matches' in which opponents attempt to puncture each other's egos through name–calling, often about the protagonists' mothers: this requires the ability to absorb and respond to highly personal comments without showing emotion. Gard (2001) argues that, while some boys avoid sports where they think the risk of injury is too high, others actively seek them out, speaking with relish about brutal body contact. This is echoed by groups of girls constructing masculine femininities. Kelly, Pomerantz and Currie (2005) found not only that stoicism in the face of injury was important to central members of communities of practice of skateboarder femininity (and, indeed, was one factor that differentiated them from those who were more peripheral), but also that the more serious skaters positively enjoyed the adrenaline rush that came with falling. Similarly, Theberge (2003) reports that many teenage female ice-hockey players not only relished the physical violence of the sport, describing their own play as 'aggressive', but also believed that they should be allowed to play by male rules, in which deliberately knocking down another player using one's body is a legitimate tactic.

For some boys, group identities are also bound up with a sense that they have to contend with violence in their local community, and that this requires toughness and willingness to fight and face danger on their own part. Cunningham and Meunier (2004) point out that the young men they studied reported often having to deal with gang or turf hassles in their local communities, suggesting that this may be related to the development of masculinities that emphasize bravado attitudes. O'Donnell and Sharpe (2000) report that fear of racial attacks was very much part of the reality of the lives of the young black men in their research. Archer and Yamashita (2003) argue that working-class urban masculinities are strongly associated with a sense of place that distinguishes 'safe' and 'unsafe' locales. The young men they studied thought of their local area as an unsafe space in which they needed to be tough to survive, but which was, for them, home territory in which they were less vulnerable to attack than if they strayed outside its boundaries. Archer (2003) found that young urban British Muslims had similar fears, but felt that they could avoid racial and other violence by being known to have 'back-up' in the form of their friends. Consequently, while masculinity is generally associated with risk and danger, in some cases this is invited and considered exciting, and in others it is related to a fear of attack against which the local community of practice of teenage masculinity constructs a hypervisible hypermasculinity in which (real or imagined) group defence and gang membership (Archer 2003) become essential both to perceptions of individual safety and to group self-esteem.

(Hetero)sexualities

The performance of (hetero)sexuality is very important to adolescents, and is central to most teenage communities of masculinity and femininity practice. For boys, the performance of heterosexuality is bound up with manhood; for girls it is at least partly about popularity. Duncan (2004) and Gulbrandsen (2003) both argue that there is an association between popularity among girls and popularity with boys, so that girls who were sought after as girlfriends for powerful boys were more likely to command social power within the wider peer group. The importance of talk about boys, Duncan suggests, means that young lesbians find it difficult to fit in with local communities of femininity practice, because they cannot contribute to this discourse. Aapola, Gonick and Harris (2005), on the other hand, argue that, while homophobia restricts bisexual and lesbian young women's recognition and expression of their sexual feelings, these can also be liberating identities, taking them outside of the confines of the mutually panoptic policing of teenage girls' sexualities.

For boys, the performance of a hypersexualized masculinity (Archer and Yamashita 2003) and predatory sexuality (Kehily 2002; Tolman *et al.*

2004) is central to demonstrating one's manhood to male peers. This is strongly bound up with the power of the male body; young men – and young women (Aapola, Gonick and Harris 2005) – with disabilities are assumed to be asexual unless they can make a clear claim to be otherwise (Martino and Pallotta-Chiarolli 2003). Kehily (2002) argues that a central theme in boys' discourses around sexual activity is that they 'know it already', and that this knowledge has been acquired through their own efforts, including sexual exploration with girlfriends. In this way, young men claim to be in control over every aspect of their sexuality and sexual behaviour. This control does not just concern one's own body but extends to the bodies of others, particularly young women: Youdell (2005) found that the teenage boys in her study assumed a right of access to girls' bodies, touching them and even moving them around in space as they wished, sometimes with the girls' apparent consent, sometimes without.

At the same time, heterosexual boys appear to see male bodies as disgusting, to the extent that they feel that they could be contaminated by their own emissions. The boys in Kehily's (2002) study said that they would not kiss a woman after she had performed oral sex on them, and while they admitted to masturbating, buying pornography for masturbatory purposes was frowned upon, as it involved seeking sex without being desired. Kehily (2002: 140) argues that 'through engagements with sex-talk, masturbation and pornography, young men *constitute* a version of heterosexuality that is associated with a desirable masculinity'. Experience of heterosexual sex gives young men kudos in the peer group: the power/knowledge acquired can be mobilized to dominate others. At the same time, Tolman *et al.* (2004) argue that boys' desires are not confined to the sexual arena: those they studied wanted relationships with girls because they would also allow them deeper emotional intimacy than was available with their other friends. Redman (2001) further reports that some boys actively construct a middle-class individualistic heterosexuality focused around romantic involvement with their girlfriends, in opposition to the perceived homosociality of their working-class peers. While such an identity allows a greater degree of feminization in male behaviour, he argues, it continues to position girls as less powerful, passive and somewhat helpless.

Homophobia remains rife among young men, with the result that they are obliged to perform heterosexuality to avoid accusations of homosexuality; Tolman *et al.* (2004) found that some boys felt so pressured into proving their heterosexuality that they had sexual experiences with girls that they later regretted. Kehily (2002) reports that the boys in her study seemed to find even talking about gay sex potentially emasculating, and having a gay friend was considered almost unimaginable. Men of South-East Asian origin were feminized by this group as weak and ineffectual because it was assumed that they could not have sex before marriage: this excluded them from legitimate participation in the local community of practice of active heterosexual masculinity.

Both boys and girls participate in virgin/whore narratives which collectively police behaviour: those who transgress the boundaries of teenage sexual propriety may not be considered to be legitimate participants in local communities of heterosexual masculinity and femininity practice. While for boys having a reputation for promiscuity could be a source of prestige and might even be something to boast about (Kehily 2002), this is emphatically not the case for girls. Archer (2003) found that British Muslim boys expected their female peers to remain modestly confined to the home and avoid boys, while they themselves frequently had white girlfriends. She argues that, for these boys, masculinity was defined through the operation of double standards in which they saw themselves as respecting the reputation of female Muslims (whose behaviour, because it reflected on the family, had to be morally unimpeachable) by confining their sexual activities to white girls.

Girls from all ethnic backgrounds are constantly subject to a panoptic gaze, from both boys and other girls, that acts to control and limit their behaviour. Such policing frequently takes place through narrative: girls who transgress the boundaries are likely to have their exploits described in florid terms. Such stories are one way in which the majority position themselves as behaving appropriately. For example, Canaan (1986) reports on a community of adolescents in the United States in which stories about one particular girl and the 'kinky sex' she had with her boyfriend were widely circulated. These tales of supposedly unnatural and immoral practices served to position the sexual activity engaged in by the majority of girls as normal, natural and morally blameless.

Lees (1993) reports that all the girls she studied were worried about their reputations. Such concern can lead girls to take constant care about how their bodies are displayed (Youdell 2005), increasing the internalization of the panoptic gaze. Such an emphasis on respectable sexuality seems to be particularly important for working-class girls, and is controlled both within communities of teenage femininity practice (Skeggs 1997; Youdell 2005) and from outside: mothers, in particular, have a role in inducting young women into the community of practice of adult feminine respectability, especially through the policing of dress (Hey 1997). Archer (2003) found that the young Muslim men in her study expected the girls in their community to wear traditional garments, arguing that to do otherwise was a sign of resistance and moral decay, though they themselves wore Western dress.

The panoptic gaze can be strongly internalized by girls in particular circumstances. Rapoport, Garb and Penso (1995) argue that the narratives of girls in an Israeli Zionist religious school were so saturated with the daily practices of modesty that they seemed obsessed. This was achieved not through overt surveillance by the school authorities, but from the mutual scrutiny of the dominant community of practice of femininity within the school, in which the behaviour of the younger girls was supervised by the older ones through daily discussion of the everyday implications of religious observance: through this the newer members of the community were seen as 'becoming moral' (Rapaport, Garb and Penso 1995: 52). In a completely different context, Weekes (2004) argues that young black British women both draw on black cultural forms, such as rap music, in their construction of black femininity, while at the same time distancing themselves from the misogynistic content of the lyrics by constructing them as derogating only other women, whose behaviour deserves such censure, thus internalizing the construction of a hierarchy of good and bad femininities.

Williams (2002) argues that for the working-class community she studied in the United States, sexual activity by young women was seen as part of growing up, and so embraced as part of a move into the community of practice of adult femininity. On the other hand, Skeggs (1997) found that the young working-class women in her British study felt shame around sex and lacked belief in their sexual feelings, and Lees (1993) reports that few of the girls she studied spoke of sexual experiences as pleasurable. Canaan (1986) found that a group of middle-class American girls not only found sex boring but blamed themselves for this. Both Lees (1993) and Youdell (2005) note that, in contrast to boys, girls are not expected to talk about sex. Indeed, Youdell (2005: 259) argues that silence can be crucial to a girl's reputation:

> A girl should not discuss her sexual activity with anyone, including friends who are girls. The greater number of boys a girl has had sex with (coitus or not), the greater the imperative for silence.
>
> The girls' moral discourse and the virgin/whore binary that it cites is not just a prohibition of sexual activity. Rather, some possibility of sexual activity is retained, although this is tightly bounded and the risk of 'slag' is ever present. In the girls' constitution of heterosexual femininities, sexual activity is only protected from the performative interpellation slag if a girl does not talk about this sexual activity. That is, feminine desire must be silenced.

Thus, teenage communities of masculinity practice construct masculinity in part through a performed and open (hetero)sexuality, while the concomitant communities of practice of femininity have a very different emphasis on a sexuality that is restricted and silenced.

Reified objects and communities of teenage masculinity and femininity practice

Reified objects, as we saw in Chapter 3, are used to mark membership of communities of practice, and they are particularly important to adolescent communities. Although they usually signify membership of communities of both boys and girls, they are used differently by males and females within these. Consequently, an examination of some of the ways in which objects become reified markers of membership is illuminating of the workings of young people's communities of practice of masculinity and femininity.

A major way in which community membership is marked among young people is through clothing and personal style. Different teenage communities wear distinctively different clothing (Kehily and Pattman 2006): again, these styles are constructed relationally, so that what is worn by one group will be anathema to another. Aapola, Gonick and Harris (2005) note that displaying a similar style can enhance girls' friendships through the sharing of markers of identity. Skeggs (1997) describes dressing up to go out as a joint venture between the young women she studied, as they tried on each other's clothes and did one another's make-up: feminine performance is thus learned by the group with and from each other. Physical attractiveness can be crucial to membership of 'cool', powerful communities (Kehily 2002). Jackson (2006) argues that popular femininities in the northern English schools she studied required prettiness (which included being thin), wearing fashionable clothes and make-up, and having the latest mobile telephones. The equivalent boys were tall, athletic and good-looking, although, again, wearing the right (expensive) clothes was another way to demonstrate 'coolness'; this was also the case in Davis's (2001) study of African-American boys. Fashionable clothing is not important for all groups, however: the 'burnouts' in Eckert's (1989) study, constructing their community in opposition to 'popular' ways of being a teenager, favoured thrift store and second-hand clothing.

The body is implicated in the construction of communities of masculinity and femininity practice not only through the way it is clothed, but also in the way it is used. Several researchers have commented on the distinctive styles of walking used by young black men, and we saw in Chapter 8 how it can cause problems for them in school (Gillborn 1990; Sewell 1997). Archer and Yamashita (2003) argue that the 'bouncing' walk typical of these groups reflects a black urban hypervisible masculinity which uses expressive and self-conscious styles deliberately to differentiate them from others. For young women, the body can function very differently. Many communities of adolescent femininity practice take up an emphasized femininity, in which the body is performed as existing for the pleasure of others and experienced through a male objectifying gaze (Kehily 2002; Aapola, Gonick and Harris 2005). Actively attempting to attract that gaze, however, may vehemently be denied, as it conflicts with the requirement, discussed above, that girls should not be overtly sexual (Gleeson and Frith 2004). While being the object of male attention can be experienced as exciting and self-confirming, the requirement for it within emphasized femininity can also be problematic: as Skeggs (1997) points out, the bodies we have may not fit what is considered to be attractive within a particular group at a particular time and place. A body that, because of its shape, size or colour, cannot perform dominant forms of masculinity and femininity, will prevent an individual from full participation in the communities of practice that value these forms. Other communities of femininity practice will, of course, explicitly reject them: the skateboarding girls studied by Kelly, Pomerantz and Currie (2005), for example, used skater styles of dress as a way of symbolizing their dissociation from emphasized femininity, favouring casual, baggy clothing and deriding girls who took trouble to make themselves look pretty.

Language and how it is used are also important ways in which groups include and exclude each other. This is partly a matter of shared repertoire. Davies (2005) notes the repeated use of Wiccan greetings by the teenage girls developing these websites. Kelly, Pomerantz and Currie's skater girls both used skater slang and made up their own, consolidating their exclusivity and difference from more hegemonic forms of femininity and marking their strong identification with skater culture. At the same time, however, they were prevented from being core members of the wider, male-dominated skater community by the use of technical terms by male skaters as an exclusionary strategy. The male working-class Londoners studied by Archer and Yamashita (2003) saw both accent and language as important defining features of their identities, to the extent that they were reluctant to change these in order to ease their entry into the labour market. Similarly, Eckert's (1989) 'burnouts' deliberately used non-standard grammar, such as multiple negatives, and had distinctive group pronunciation patterns.

For oppositional communities, there are some shared objects that are particularly salient to the construction of identity against dominant norms. Music can be important in this respect, with forms of black or alternative music repeatedly mentioned in the literature (Weekes 2004; Kelly, Pomerantz and Currie 2005). Archer (2003) reports that the Muslim boys she studied were especially scathing about South-East Asian music, which they associated with femininity, pouring particular scorn on Bollywood musicals. They preferred to consolidate their masculinities by listening to music associated with black American males.

Smoking and drinking can be important markers of belonging to specific communities of masculinity and femininity practice, from the point of view of both insiders and outsiders. Jackson (2006) observes that both smoking and drinking are important in the construction, both by the girls themselves and by the media, of a masculine 'ladette' identity. Both Eckert (1989) and Cullen (2006) note the use of cigarette smoking as part of particular masculinities and femininities, and its importance as a way of securing and consolidating friendship. For Eckert's 'burnouts', smoking both cigarettes and cannabis was part of their oppositional positioning and claims to adult status, but the sharing of cigarettes was also an important way of acting as a loyal community member, particularly as sharing generally was a central aspect of 'burnout' identity. Cullen (2006) argues that such mutual gift-giving is centrally important to young women's social networks, to the extent that being in a position to share cigarettes becomes a significant marker of membership in a community of practice. Furthermore, she suggests, as girls smoke more, addiction itself becomes an important symbolic bond:

> For Jody and Lisa [aged 14 and 15], cigarettes punctuate the tedium of the long school day and demonstrate their resistance to school authority. The young women reproduced this close social bond as they bantered about the types of cigarette they liked to smoke, and the urgency ... to conclude the interview in order to go for another smoke.
>
> (Cullen 2006: 9)

Indeed, cigarette smoking was so important to the identity construction of the young women in Cullen's study, that different brands had become significant markers of membership of different communities of femininity practice.

Such gift-giving is common to communities of femininity practice, where they seem to be particularly significant and may relate to the importance of caring identities. Cullen (2006: 2) records that the young women she studied shared 'snacks, music files, clothes, text messages, mobile phone credit and photographs'. Kehily (2002) notes that girls share magazines. Aapola, Gonick and Harris (2005) observe that girls give each other stereotypically feminine gifts of cuddly toys and cosmetic products: they argue that these symbolize the value that girls place on friendship. Objects in general seem to be more important to femininities than to masculinities. For example, Davies (2005) found that teenage Wiccan websites invariably showed pictures of the girls' altars: owning an altar and knowing how to arrange it were important markers of membership of this particular community.

Finally, space and how it is used operate as significant markers of membership of particular communities of practice, some of which are strongly masculine or feminine. McRobbie (1991) notes the importance of the bedroom as a location for the construction of identity for younger teenage girls, while Cullen (2005) argues that, for older young people, particular outdoor spaces (playgrounds, cemeteries) can be considered to be the territory of specific groups over several years. Archer (2003) reports that the young South-East Asian men she studied laid emphasis on the active, outdoor nature of their lives, understanding them in contrast to those of their female peers, who were expected to stay indoors: masculinity is here directly associated with spatial freedom.

Both Eckert (1989) and Cullen (2005) observe that different areas within educational institutions may be colonized by one group and therefore avoided by others. In the further education college where Cullen carried out some of her fieldwork, 'the *common room* was seen by young people in the college as a hang out for "grungers" and "gays", in contrast to the working-class Black British "rudie" straight cultural space of *the refectory*' (Cullen 2005: 5, emphasis in original). Similarly, the 'jocks' in Eckert's study used the cafeteria, which was avoided by the 'burnouts', who hung out in the courtyard next to it, with the result that this space was avoided by 'jocks', even though it provided a convenient short-cut between classes. In these ways, space and how it is used become strongly reified as markers of community membership in related but often different ways for male and female participants.

Conclusion

It is clear from what has been discussed in this chapter that adolescent communities of masculinity and femininity practice construct their group identities in multitudinous ways. Most significant in this is that adolescence is very much a process of becoming: as they traverse it, young people are very surely moving towards adulthood. As they work out what sort of adult they want to be, they try on different identities and ways of behaving, attempting to construct and discover the possibilities for themselves as adults, while at the same time fully participating in their local peer communities. Indeed, while there is a constant looking forward towards adulthood, it is at this age that peer communities become overwhelmingly important to identity.

Because the question 'what sort of person am I?' is so salient at this point, the concomitant issue of who one is not looms large in young people's communal and individual self-constructions. This means that there is much greater refinement of group identities and splitting into small, subcultural communities, so that being *this* type of person is clearly differentiated from being *that* type. This takes place through a constant and repeated Othering of outsiders, so that their ways of being become strongly antithetical to members of any particular community. How one does not conduct one's life, thus, becomes as important as how one does; there is a constant policing of thought and behaviour in a mutually panoptic system of boundary construction and reinforcement.

These strongly differentiated communities of practice of masculinity and femininity are of enormous importance to young people's futures: they really do serve to construct the adults that they are soon to become. The adolescents of Kehily and Pattman (2006) and Redman's (2001) studies, who worked hard to differentiate themselves from the working-class 'dropouts' or homosocial 'lads' they felt they had left behind, will be able to use these aspects of their communities of practice to prepare themselves for success in wider society. The middle-class young women studied by Williams (2002), whose focus on competitive sports led them to compete both with each other and with boys, are gaining skills and dispositions that will stand them in good stead if they wish later to enter corporate society. Meanwhile, Archer and Yamashita's (2003) Harkton boys, with their valorization of working-class, urban styles of speech, clothing and demeanour and strong affiliation to their local area, are preparing themselves mainly for social exclusion as surely as Willis's (1977) lads did. By treating as anathema and inauthentic even the minimal changes they would need to make, to make themselves suitable for the local labour market or for further education, they condemn themselves to social immobility and disadvantage. Adolescent communities of masculinity and feminity practice prepare their members for concomitant adult communities, and the separations in the former form the foundations for further differences in the latter.

Interventions

Given that differences between adolescent communities of masculinity and femininity practice are so important to life chances later on, interventions at this point need, as far as possible, to encourage an openness to alternatives and, if possible, membership of multiple communities.

- Many young people are members of different communities of masculinity and femininity practice in different locations or situations. This gives them a wider number of ways to be, while also supporting the transition to adulthood. Such multiple memberships can be fostered by encouraging young people to take part in a range of activities, such as sports, that take them beyond local friendship groups.
- For younger teenagers, the trying-on of identity is particularly important. Again, a range of activities in different locations with different groups should be encouraged in order to make this easier.
- It may be possible, through discussions with young people about the operation of the panoptic gaze, to help them to find points of resistance to it, individually or collectively.
- Given the importance of danger to masculinity, it is likely that many young men and some young women will seek it out. In order to avoid the concomitant higher rate of injury and death among young men (Connell 1995), attempts should be made to provide the thrills that are associated with this but in safer circumstances, perhaps by providing more outdoor and adventurous activities for young people, or simply by giving them more opportunities to take part in things that feel more dangerous than they are. It is better that they should be experiencing the thrill that comes from falling off a speeding skateboard than that which comes from falling off a speeding motorbike.

10 Conclusion

'The boasting boys,' said Louis, 'have gone now in a vast team to play
cricket. They have driven off in their great brake, singing in chorus.
All their heads turn simultaneously at the corner by the laurel
bushes. Now they are boasting. Larpent's brother played football for
Oxford; Smith's father made a century at Lords. Archie and Hugh;
Parker and Dalton; Larpent and Smith; then again Archie and Hugh;
Parker and Dalton, Larpent and Smith – the names repeat
themselves; the names are the same always. They are the volunteers;
they are the cricketers; they are the officers of the Natural History
Society. They are always forming into fours and marching in troops
with badges on their caps; they salute simultaneously passing the
figure of their general. How majestic is their order, how beautiful is
their obedience! If I could follow, if I could be with them, I would
sacrifice all I know. But they also leave butterflies trembling with
their wings pinched off; they throw dirty pocket-handkerchiefs
clotted with blood screwed up into corners. They make little boys
sob in dark passages. They have big red ears that stand out under
their caps. Yet that is what we wish to be, Neville and I'.

(Woolf 1977: 31–2)

This book came about because I was puzzled by the question: if gender is
performative, as Butler (1990, 1993) argues, how do we know what to
perform, and does this change according to circumstances? It did not
seem to me that we are able just to choose who we are, to perform
anyone we want, so I wanted to know what the constraints were on
performance, and where they came from. My conclusion, that how to
'do' man or woman, boy or girl, is learned and constructed within local
communities of masculinity and femininity practice, is what I have been
explaining, expanding and exploring in the previous nine chapters.

Theoretically, such an idea is relatively straightforward. The key
issues that arose for me, in applying Lave and Wenger's work in this area
(Lave and Wenger 1991; Wenger 1998) specifically to questions of
gender, were the questions of the role of power/knowledge relations
within communities of practice, and of how an individual's participation
is recognized as legitimate. In developing my understanding of these
within the specific context of communities of masculinity and

femininity practice, I hope that I have taken the general theorization in this area further forward. It seems to me that without a clear understanding of how power/knowledge operates within communities, in relation to the negotiation of practice and the conferral, or otherwise, of legitimacy, the concept is significantly weakened. If, as Foucault (1982: 223) argues, 'there cannot be a society without power relations', then we have to ensure that, in conceptualizing communities of practice as central to the construction of such a fundamental aspect of identity as our maleness or femaleness, we develop a full theorisation of how power/ knowledge relations operate in this context. In particular, we need to understand how processes of mutual panoptic observation operate within communities of masculinity and femininity practice, especially at points in the life course at which boundary maintenance becomes highly salient.

This theorization having been achieved, however, it was important to see how it might work in practice, and this is what I did in Chapters 4 to 9, drawing on both my own work and that of other researchers to examine some of the processes through which children and young people construct their own identities as male and female through local communities of practice. This detail is important, because it is in the specificities of practice and the power/knowledge relations that surround it that we develop our ideas about what it is to be male and female, take these on as aspects of identity, and perform them to ourselves and others. I have demonstrated that the salience of different communities varies throughout a child's life, starting with a close focus on the family, but with the peer group and institutions, such as the school, having increasing relevance. While I have considered each of these in different ways and with respect to the various stages of a child's life, they all operate continuously and in interrelationship with each other, providing children with varied and overlapping communities of masculinity and femininity practice within which they develop their ideas about who they are.

The process through which a baby becomes a boy or girl, and then a man or woman, with all that this implies, is a long and complex one. One of the things that I have established in this book is that it is fundamentally social. It is also inherently cognitive, as children learn, through observation of others and participation in communities of practice of masculinity and femininity, what it is to be male and female in their specific local contexts. Thus the learning of what it is to be male or female is not a matter of imposition of a set of ideas or ways of behaving, but instead is a co-construction of identity, in which the child plays a central part in some communities, and a more peripheral one in others, moving between them according to location and circumstances and over time.

The construction and performance of masculinity and femininity through communities of practice, while embodied, is not governed by the body, or by the genes and hormones that make our bodily forms the way they are. While the body is crucially important to identity and how it is constructed, it is not important in the ways in which it is often perceived to be. It is not that hormones and genes, or the physical differences that these give rise to, directly affect our behaviour, but that the bodies that result can affect the possibilities of our performances and participation, in ways that are self-reinforcing. Certain communities of masculinity and femininity practice will only allow membership of those with particular bodily forms, and the practices of these communities are frequently such that these forms (through the development of particular muscle groups or styles of performance) are perpetuated, and the physical differences between them and members of other groups are increased.

Central to the idea that individual masculinities and femininities are constructed within communities of masculinity and femininity practice is the local nature of this construction. Communities of practice operate as communities at least in part because of proximity between the members. This nearness of encounter does not have to be spatial, as we saw with the online teenage Wiccan communities in Chapter 9, but there does have to be regular and frequent meeting, to enable the continuous construction and negotiation of the forms of masculinity and femininity that are central to a particular group, and the induction of new or recent members into these through legitimate peripheral participation.

Because of the local nature of participation, every community of masculinity or femininity practice is different: while we can find commonalities between groups, there will be subtle and not so subtle variations. Research into these communities, therefore, has to be detailed and small-scale, with generalizations developed from the bringing together and comparing of different studies, which may not necessarily all employ this theoretical framework. For any individual study, all we can say is that this particular community of masculinity or femininity practice is configured in these specific ways, and then consider whether other communities are similar or different.

The idea that masculinities and femininities are learned, constructed and performed through community induction and negotiation processes has some fundamental implications. The first is that, of course, what is learned could be different. This is why I have outlined possible intervention strategies at the end of each chapter. We should not be satisfied simply with understanding what children construct as funda-mental to being a boy or girl, man or woman: we can and should consider whether we really want them to think in these ways and, if necessary, work to change them. Such conceptualizations both depend upon and construct power/knowledge relations that are unequal between males and females. This is why understanding gendered power/knowledge relations as fundamental within and between communities of masculinity and femininity practice is so important.

In thinking about how we can change things we need to be clear that the sense of belonging, which comes from full participation in any community of practice, is very powerful. Consequently, communities of practice, particularly those, such as the ones I have discussed in this book, which are fundamentally bound up with identity, will have an inevitable degree of in-built inertia. It is hard to change local communities of practice, because those at the centre, who have the strongest voices when negotiating what is possible, feel comfortable there. This situation is exacerbated in the case of child communities of masculinity and femininity practice, because in some periods of childhood there is a high degree of uncertainty about what it is to be male or female, which makes children cling harder to the stereotypical views well established in their local child communities, if not in those of the adults around them. In particular, children feel the need to draw strong boundaries between groups, expecting differences to be very clear-cut so that there is as little uncertainty as possible about their own and others' positions.

If we want to have a fairer society, in which men and women, boys and girls have the freedom to take up and perform masculinities and femininities of much greater range and scope than is currently the case, we need to find ways of intervening in local communities of masculinity and femininity practice, to undermine the dominance of particular ways of being and provide alternative conceptions of what it might mean to be a man or woman. Because of the local nature of communities of masculinity and femininity practice, this means that we need to work with those communities of which we are ourselves members or with which we have frequent interactions. We need to uncover how power/ knowledge relations operate in relation to the construction of masculinities and femininities in these specific communities, and then look for, and work with, the points of resistance. By understanding the modes by which particular communities operate, we can consider how they can be changed.

In this, it is not just that the personal is political, as in the feminizt slogan, but that the political is personal. While structural social change towards greater equality is essential, it will make little difference to people's everyday lives if we do not also work within our communities of masculinity and femininity practice to alter not only how we think about ourselves but also how we practise and perform our identities in relation to others. We all, all of the time, construct our own masculinities and femininities in local communities of practice, and we support our own children and the children with whom we work or play, in doing the same. If we want those children to be able to resist the constraints on their identities, and hence their future possibilities, then we have to examine ourselves, as central members of our own communities, and consider whether our own practices act to support this. It is through small, local changes, specific, local resistances, that we can gradually build a world in which all of the possibilities for individual masculinities and femininities can be taken up by anyone, regardless of location and community membership. It is my hope that in this book, I have provided some of the theoretical and practical tools to make this possible.

References

Aapola, S., Gonick, M. and Harris, A. (2005) *Young Femininity: Girlhood, power and social change*. Basingstoke: Palgrave Macmillan.

Adler, P.A., Kless, S.J. and Adler, P. (1992) Socialization to gender roles: popularity among elementary school boys and girls, *Sociology of Education* 65(3): 169–87.

Ali, S. (2002) Friendship and fandom: ethnicity, power and gendering, *Discourse* 23(2): 153–65.

Allen, J. (2003) *Lost Geographies of Power*. Oxford: Basil Blackwell.

Archer, L. (2003) *Race, Masculinity and Schooling*. Maidenhead: Open University Press.

Archer, L. and Yamashita, H. (2003) Theorizing inner-city masculinities: 'race', class, gender and education, *Gender and Education* 15(2): 115–32.

Attar, D. (1990). *Wasting Girls' Time: The history and politics of home economics*. London: Virago Press.

Barnes, J. (1980) *Metroland*. London: Picador.

Bem, S.L. (1998) *An Unconventional Family*. New Haven, CT: Yale University Press.

Benjamin, S. (2003) Gender and special educational needs, in C. Skelton and B. Francis (eds) *Boys and Girls in the Primary Classroom*. Maidenhead: Open University Press.

Bhana, D. (2002) Making gender in early schooling. A multi-sited ethnography of power and discourse: from Grade One to Two in Durban. Unpublished PhD thesis, University of Natal, Durban.

Bhana, D. (2005a) 'Show me the panties': girls play games in the school ground, in C. Mitchell and J. Reid-Walsh (eds) *Seven Going on Seventeen*. New York, NY: Peter Lang.

Bhana, D. (2005b) What matters to boys and girls in a black primary school in South Africa, *Early Child Development and Care* 175(2): 99–111.

Birke, L. (1999) *Feminism and the Biological Body*. Edinburgh: Edinburgh University Press.

Blaise, M. (2005) *Playing it Straight: Uncovering gender discourses in the early childhood classroom*. New York, NY: Routledge.

Bordo, S. (1993) Feminism, Foucault and the politics of the body, in C. Ramazanoğlu (ed.) *Up against Foucault*. London: Routledge.

Bourdieu, P. (1991) *Language and Symbolic Power*. Cambridge, MA: Harvard University Press.

Bourdieu, P. (2001) *Masculine Domination*. Cambridge: Polity Press.

Braidotti, R. (2002) *Metamorphoses: Towards a materialist theory of becoming*. Cambridge: Polity Press.

Briggs, H. (2000) 'Gender-bender' fish problem widens. http//news.bbc.co.uk/1/hi/in_depth/sci_tech/2000/festival_of_science/913273.stm (accessed 13 January 2005)

Brown, D. and Rich, E. (2002) Gender positioning as pedagogical practice in teaching physical education, in D. Penney (ed.) *Gender and Physical Education: Contemporary issues and future directions*. London: Routledge.

Brown, L.M. and Gilligan, C. (1993) Meeting at the crossroads: women's psychology and girls' development, *Feminism and Psychology* 3(1): 11–35.

Browne, N. (2004) *Gender Equity in the Early Years*. Maidenhead: Open University Press.

Burman, E. (1994) *Deconstructing Developmental Psychology*. London: Routledge.

Burman, E. (1995) 'What is it?' Masculinity and femininity in cultural representations of childhood, in S. Wilkinson and C. Kitzinger (eds) *Feminism and Discourse*. London: Sage.

Butler, J. (1990) *Gender Trouble: Feminism and the subversion of identity*. London: Routledge.

Butler, J. (1993) *Bodies that Matter: On the discursive limits of 'sex'*. London: Routledge.

Butler, J. (2004) *Undoing Gender*. New York, NY: Routledge.

Canaan, J. (1986) Why a 'slut' is a 'slut': cautionary tales of middle-class teenage girls' morality, in H. Varenne (ed.) *Symbolizing America*. Lincoln, NE: University of Nebraska Press.

Chapman, A. (2001) Maths talk is boys' talk: constructing masculinity in school mathematics, in W. Martino and B. Meyenn (eds) *What about the Boys? Issues of masculinity in schools*. Buckingham: Open University Press.

Cho, M.K. (2000) Bodily regulation and vocational schooling, *Gender and Education* 12(2): 149–64.

Clark, S. and Paechter, C. (2007). Tomboy identities: 'Why can't girls play football?' Gender dynamics and the playground, *Sport, Education and Society*.

Clarke, G. (1997) Playing a part: the lives of women physical education teachers, in G. Clarke and B. Humberstone (eds) *Researching Women and Sport*. Basingstoke: Macmillan Press.

Cockburn, C. (1999) 'The trouble with girls ...' A study of teenage girls' magazines in relation to sport and PE, *British Journal of Physical Education* 30(3): 11–5.

Connell, R.W. (1987) *Gender and Power*. Cambridge: Polity Press.

Connell, R.W. (1995) *Masculinities*. Cambridge: Polity Press.

Connell, R.W. (2002) *Gender*. Cambridge: Polity Press.

Connolly, P. (1998) *Racism, Gender Identities and Young Children*. London: Routledge.

Connolly, P. (2003) Gendered and gendering spaces: playgrounds in the early years, in C. Skelton and B. Francis (eds) *Boys and Girls in the Primary Classroom*. Maidenhead: Open University Press.

Connolly, P. (2004) *Boys and Schooling in the Early Years*. London: RoutledgeFalmer.

Cullen, F. (2005) Cotching in the cotch: Young women, embodied geographies and transition. Paper presented to the Gender and Education 5th International Conference, University of Cardiff, Cardiff, March.

Cullen, F. (2006) 'Two's up and poncing fags': Young women's smoking practices and gift exchange. Paper presented to the ESRC-funded seminar series: Girls and Education 3–16, University of Lancaster, June.

Cunningham, M. and Meunier, L.N. (2004) The influence of peer experiences on bravado attitudes among African American males, in N. Way and J. Y. Chu (eds) *Adolescent Boys: Exploring diverse cultures of boyhood*. New York, NY: New York University Press.

Damasio, A.R. (1994) *Descartes' Error: Emotion, reason and the human brain*. London: Picador.

Davies, B. (1989) *Frogs and Snails and Feminist Tales: Preschool children and gender*. Sydney: Allen & Unwin.

Davies, B. (2003) *Shards of Glass*. Cresshill, NJ: Hampton Press.

Davies, J. (2005) Weaving magic webs: Internet identities and teen Wiccan subcultures. A consideration of a particular on line community and their web-based interactions. http//www.shef. ac.uk/content/1/c6/05/05/23/davies_1.pdf (accessed 12 July 2006).

Davis, J.E. (2001) Transgressing the masculine: African American boys and the future of schools, in W. Martino and B. Meyenn (eds) *What about the Boys? Issues of masculinity in schools*. Buckingham: Open University Press.

Delamont, S. (1994) Accentuating the positive: refocusing the research on girls and science, *Studies in Science Education* 23: 59–74.

Department for Education and Employment (1998a) *The Implementation of the National Numeracy Strategy*. Sudbury: DfEE Publications.

Department for Education and Employment (1998b) *The National Literacy Strategy*. Sudbury: DfEE Publications.

Department for Education and Employment (1999) *Physical Education.* London: Department for Education and Employment/Qualifications and Curriculum Authority.

Department for Education and Skills (2004) *Sex and Relationship Education – Schools' Responsibilities.* London: Department for Education and Skills.

Department for Education and Skills (2006a) GCSE and equivalent results for young people in England, 2005/06 (Provisional). http// www.dfes.gov.uk/rsgateway/DB/SFR/s000688/index.shtml (accessed 23 November 2006).

Department for Education and Skills (2006b) GCSE/VCE A/AS examination results for young people in England, 2005/06 (Provisional). http//www.dfes.gov.uk/rsgateway/DB/SFR/s000687/index.shtml (accessed 23 November 2006).

Descartes, R. (1968) *Discourse on Method and the Meditations.* Harmondsworth: Penguin.

Dixon, C. (1997) Pete's tool: identity and sex-play in the design and technology classroom, *Gender and Education* 9(1): 89–104.

Donath, J.S. (1999) Identity and deception in the virtual community, in M.A. Smith and P. Kollock (eds) *Communities in Cyberspace.* London: Routledge.

Dreger, A. (1995–2005) Shifting the paradigm of intersex treatment. http://www.isna.org/compare/ (accessed 19 March 2003).

Dryden, C. (1999) *Being Married, Doing Gender.* London: Routledge.

Duncan, N. (2004) It's important to be nice, but it's nicer to be important: girls, popularity and sexual competition, *Sex Education* 4(2): 137–52.

Dunne, G.A. (1997). *Lesbian Lifestyles: Women's work and the politics of sexuality.* Basingstoke: Macmillan.

Dyhouse, C. (1976) Social Darwinistic ideas and the development of women's education 1880–1920, *History of Education* 5(1): 41–58.

Dyhouse, C. (1977) Good wives and little mothers: social anxieties and the schoolgirl's curriculum 1890–1920, *Oxford Review of Education* 3(1): 21–35.

Dyhouse, C. (1978) Towards a 'feminine' curriculum for English schoolgirls: the demands of ideology 1870–1963, *Womens' Studies International Quarterly* 1: 291–311.

Eckert, P. (1989). *Jocks and Burnouts: Social categories and identity in the high school.* New York, NY: Teachers College Press.

Eckert, P. and McConnell-Ginet, S. (1992) Think practically and look locally: language and gender as community-based practice, *Annual Review of Anthropology* 21: 461–90.

Epstein, D. (1999) Sex play: romantic significations, sexism and silences in the schoolyard, in D. Epstein and J.T. Sears (eds) *A Dangerous Knowing: Sexuality, pedagogy and popular culture*. London: Cassell.

Epstein, D. and Johnson, R. (1994) On the straight and narrow: the heterosexual presumption, homophobias and schools, in D. Epstein (ed.) *Challenging Lesbian and Gay Inequalities in Education*. Buckingham: Open University Press.

Epstein, D. and Johnson, R. (1998). *Schooling Sexualities*. Buckingham: Open University Press.

Epstein, D., Kehily, M., Mac an Ghaill, M. and Redman, P. (2001) Boys and girls come out to play: making masculinities and femininities in school playgrounds, *Men and Masculinities* 4(2): 158–72.

Equal Opportunities Commission (1999) Gender issues in vocational training and workplace achievement of 14–19-year-olds: an EOC perspective, *The Curriculum Journal* 10(2): 209–29.

Equal Opportunities Commission (2001) *Sex Stereotyping: From school to work*. Manchester: Equal Opportunities Commission.

Equal Opportunities Commission (2002) *Response to the Green Paper, 14–19: Extending opportunities, raising standards*. London: Equal Opportunities Commission.

Evaldson, A-C. (2003) Throwing like a girl? Situating gender differences in physicality across game contexts, *Childhood* 10(4): 475–97.

Evans, J., Rich, E. and Holroyd, R. (2004) Disordered eating and disordered schooling: what schools do to middle-class girls, *British Journal of Sociology of Education* 25(2): 123–42.

Fausto-Sterling, A. (1987) Society writes biology/biology constructs gender, *Daedalus* 116: 61–76.

Fausto-Sterling, A. (1989) Life in the XY corral, *Women's Studies International Forum* 12(3): 319–31.

Fausto-Sterling, A. (1993) The five sexes: why male and female are not enough, *The Sciences*, March/April: 20–4.

Fausto-Sterling, A. (2000a) The five sexes, revisited, *The Sciences* 40(4): 18–23.

Fausto-Sterling, A. (2000b) *Sexing the Body: Gender politics and the construction of sexuality*. New York, NY: Basic Books.

Fitzclarence, L. and Hickey, C. (2001) Real footballers don't eat quiche: old narratives in new times, *Men and Masculinities* 4(2): 118–39.

Fletcher, S. (1984) *Women First*. London: Athlone Press.

Fordham, S. (1996) *Blacked Out: Dilemmas of race, identity and success at Capital High*. Chicago, IL: University of Chicago Press.

Foucault, M. (1963) *The Birth of the Clinic*. London: Routledge.

Foucault, M. (1972) *The Archaeology of Knowledge*. London: Tavistock.

Foucault, M. (1977) *Discipline and Punish*. London: Penguin.

Foucault, M. (1978) *The History of Sexuality Volume One*. London: Penguin.

Foucault, M. (1979a) Interview with Lucette Finas, in M. Morris and P. Patton (eds) *Michel Foucault: Power, Truth, Strategy*. Sydney: Feral Publications.

Foucault, M. (1979b) Power and norm: notes, in M. Morris and P. Patton (eds) *Michel Foucault: Power, Truth, Strategy*. Sydney: Feral Publications.

Foucault, M. (1980) *Power/Knowledge: Selected interviews and other writings 1972-1977*. Hemel Hempstead: Harvester Press.

Foucault, M. (1982) The subject and power, in H.L. Dreyfus and P. Rabinov (eds) *Michel Foucault: Beyond structuralism and hermeneutics*. Brighton: Harvester Press.

Foucault, M. (1988a) Technologies of the self, in L.H. Martin, H. Gutman and P. H. Hutton (eds) *Technologies of the Self: A seminar with Michel Foucault*. Amherst, MA: University of Massachusetts Press.

Foucault, M. (1988b) *Politics, Philosophy, Culture: Interviews and other writings 1977-1984*. London: Routledge.

Francis, B. (1998) *Power Plays: Primary school children's conception of gender, power and adult work*. Stoke-on-Trent: Trentham Books.

Francis, B. (2000) *Boys, Girls and Achievement: Addressing the classroom issues*. London: RoutledgeFalmer.

Frosh, S., Phoenix, A. and Pattman, R. (2002) *Young Masculinities: Understanding boys in contemporary society*. Basingstoke: Palgrave.

Gallas, K. (1998) *'Sometimes I Can Be Anything': Power, gender and identity in a primary classroom*. New York, NY: Teachers College Press.

Gard, M. (2001) 'I like smashing people and I like getting smashed myself': addressing issues of masculinity in physical education and sport, in W. Martino and B. Meyenn (eds) *What about the Boys? Issues of masculinity in schools*. Buckingham: Open University Press.

Gaskell, J. (1995) Making it work: gender and vocational education, in J. Gaskell and J. Willinsky (eds) *Gender In/forms Curriculum*. New York, NY: Teachers College Press.

Gatens, M. (1991) *Feminism and Philosophy: Perspectives on difference and equality*. Cambridge: Polity Press.

Gelman, S.A., Taylor, M.G. and Nguyen, S.P. (2004) Mother–child conversations about gender: understanding the acquisition of essentialist beliefs, *Monographs of the Society for Research in Child Development* 69(1).

George, R. (2004) The importance of friendship during primary to secondary school transfer, in M. Benn and C. Chitty (eds) *A Tribute to Caroline Benn: Education and democracy*. London: Continuum.

George, R. (2006) Black girls, schooling and friendship. Paper presented to the ESRC-funded seminar series: Girls and Education 3–16, University of Lancaster, June.

Gillborn, D. (1990) *'Race', Ethnicity and Education*. London: Unwin Hyman.

Gleeson, K. and Frith, H. (2004) Pretty in pink: young women presenting mature sexual identities, in A. Harris (ed.) *All about the Girl: Culture, power and identity*. London: Routledge.

Goffman, E. (1976) *Gender Advertisements*. London: Macmillan.

Gordon, T., Holland, J., Lahelma, E. and Thomson, R. (2005) Imagining gendered adulthood: anxiety, ambivalence, avoidance and anticipation, *European Journal of Women's Studies* 12(1): 83–103.

Gore, J. (1998) Disciplining bodies: on the continuity of power relations in pedagogy, in T.S. Popkewitz and M. Brennan (eds) *Foucault's Challenge: Discourse, power and knowledge in education*. Columbia University, NY: Teachers College Press.

Gramsci, A. (1971) *Selections from the Prison Notebooks of Antonio Gramsci*. London: Lawrence and Wishart.

Griffin, P. (1991) Identity management strategies among lesbian and gay educators, *Qualitative Studies in Education* 4(3): 189–202.

Griffiths, V. (1995) *Adolescent Girls and Their Friends: A feminizt ethnography*. Aldershot: Avebury.

Gulbrandsen, M. (2003) Peer relations as arenas for gender constructions among teenagers, *Pedagogy, Culture and Society* 11(1): 113–31.

Haavind, H. (2003) Masculinity by rule-breaking: cultural contestations in the transitional move from being a child to being a young male, *NORA: Nordic Journal of Women's Studies* 11(2): 89–100.

Hacking, I. (1995) *Rewriting the Soul: Multiple personality and the science of memory*. Princeton, NJ: Princeton University Press.

Halberstam, J. (1998) *Female Masculinity*. Durham, NC: Duke University Press.

Härkönen, U. (1995) Written text conceptions of female child care personnel about girls' and boys' work and mothers' and fathers' work education. Education Resources Information Center (ERIC) no. ED389466. http://www.eric.ed.gov/sitemap html_0900000b8012 de1a.html (accessed 2 May 2006).

Harris, J.R. (1998) *The Nurture Assumption: Why children turn out the way they do*. London: Bloomsbury.

Harris, M. (1999) *Gender Sensitivity in Primary School Mathematics*. London: Commonwealth Secretariat.

Harris, J. and Penney, D. (2002) Gender, health and physical education. In D. Penney (ed.) *Gender and Physical Education: Contemporary issues and future directions*. London: Routledge.

Hawkins, A.J., Marshall, C.M. and Allen, S.M. (1998) The orientation towards domestic labour questionnaire: exploring dual-earner wives' sense of fairness about family work, *Journal of Family Psychology* 12(2): 244–58.

Head, J. (1997) *Working with Adolescents: Constructing identity*. London: Falmer Press.

Hekman, S.J. (1995) *Moral Voices, Moral Selves: Carol Gilligan and feminizt moral theory*. Cambridge: Polity Press.

Hey, V. (1997) *The Company She Keeps: An ethnography of girls' friendship*. Buckingham: Open University Press.

Hey, V., Creese, A., Daniels, H., Fielding, S. and Leonard, D. (2001) 'Sad, bad or sexy boys': girls' talk in and out of the classroom, in W. Martino and B. Meyenn (eds) *What about the Boys? Issues of masculinity in schools*. Buckingham: Open University Press.

Holloway, W. (1994) Separation, integration and difference: contradictions in a gender regime, in H.L. Radtke and H.J. Stam (eds) *Power/Gender*. London: Sage.

hooks, b. (1982) *Ain't I a Woman: Black women and feminizm*. London: Pluto Press.

Intersex Society of North America (1995–2003) http://www.isna.org/faq/third-gender (accessed 19 March 2003).

Ivinson, G. and Murphy, P. (2003) Boys don't write romance: the construction of knowledge and social gender identities in English classrooms, *Pedagogy, Culture and Society* 11(1): 89–111.

Jackson, C. (2006) *Lads and Ladettes in School: Gender and a fear of failure*. Maidenhead: Open University Press.

Jackson, C. and Warin, J. (2000) The importance of gender as an aspect of identity at key transition points in compulsory education, *British Educational Research Journal* 26(3): 375–91.

Jackson, S. and Gee, S. (2005) 'Look Janet', 'No you look John': Constructions of gender in early school reader illustrations across 50 years, *Gender and Education* 17(2): 115–28.

Jenson, J., de Castell, S. and Bryson, M. (2003) 'Girl talk': Gender, equity and identity discourses in a school-based computer culture, *Women's Studies International Forum* 26(6): 561–73.

Jones, S. and Myhill, D. (2004a) Seeing things differently: teachers' constructions of underachievement, *Gender and Education* 16(4): 531–46.

Jones, S. and Myhill, D. (2004b) 'Troublesome boys' and 'compliant girls': gender identity and perceptions of achievement and underachievement, *British Journal of Sociology of Education* 25(5): 547–61.

Jordan, E. (1995) Fighting boys and fantasy play: the construction of masculinity in the early years of school, *Gender and Education* 7(1): 69–86.

Karraker, K.H., Vogel, D.A. and Lake, M.A. (1995) Parents' gender-stereotyped perceptions of newborns: the eye of the beholder revisited, *Sex Roles* 33(9/10): 687–701.

Karsten, L. (2003) Children's use of public space: the gendered world of the playground, *Childhood* 10(4): 457–73.

Keddie, N. (1971) Classroom knowledge. In M.F.D. Young (ed.) *Knowledge and Control*. West Drayton: Macmillan.

Kehily, M.J. (2002) *Sexuality, Gender and Schooling: Shifting agendas in social learning*. London: RoutledgeFalmer.

Kehily, M. J. and Pattman, R. (2006) Middle-class struggle? Identity-work and leisure among sixth formers in the United Kingdom, *British Journal of Sociology of Education* 27(1): 37–52.

Kehily, M.J., Mac an Ghaill, M., Epstein, D. and Redman, P. (2002) Private girls and public worlds: producing femininities in the primary school, *Discourse* 23(2): 167–77.

Kelly, D.M., Pomerantz, S. and Currie, D. (2005) Skater girlhood and emphasized femininity: 'you can't land an ollie properly in heels', *Gender and Education* 17(3): 229–48.

Kessler, S. (1990) The medical construction of gender: case management of intersexed infants, *Signs: Journal of Women in Culture and Society* 16(1): 3–26.

Kessler, S. (1998) *Lessons from the Intersexed*. New Brunswick, NJ: Rutgers University Press.

Kessler, S. and McKenna, W. (1978) *Gender: An ethnomethodological approach*. New York, NY: Wiley.

Koyama, E. (1995–2003) Suggested guidelines for non-intersex individuals writing about intersexuality and intersex people. http://www.intersexinitiative.org/articles/writing-guidelines.html (accessed 19 March 2003).

Kraus, K. and Carter, P.A. (2004) Disincentives to employment: family and educational policies in unified Germany, in R.D. Lakes and P.A. Carter (eds) *Globalizing Education for Work: Comparative perspectives on gender and the new economy*. Mahwah, NJ: Lawrence Erlbaum.

Lakes, R.D. (2004) Working-class masculinities and femininities: new considerations for vocational education, in R.D. Lakes and P.A. Carter (eds) *Globalizing Education for Work: Comparative perspectives on gender and the new economy*. Mahwah, NJ: Lawrence Erlbaum.

Laqueur, T. (1990) *Making Sex: Body and gender from the Greeks to Freud*. Cambridge, MA: Harvard University Press.

Lave, J. and Wenger, E. (1991) *Situated Learning: Legitimate peripheral participation*. Cambridge: Cambridge University Press.

Lee, H. (2000) *To Kill a Mockingbird*. London: Vintage. First published in 1990.

Lees, S. (1993) *Sugar and Spice: Sexuality and adolescent girls*. London: Penguin.

Leroi, A.M. (2003) *Mutants: On the form, varieties and errors of the human body*. London: HarperCollins.

Letts, W. (2001) Boys will be boys (if they pay attention in science class), in W. Martino and B. Meyenn (eds) *What about the Boys? Issues of masculinity in schools*. Buckingham: Open University Press.

Lloyd, B. and Duveen, G. (1992). *Gender Identities and Education: The impact of starting school*. Hemel Hempstead: Harvester Press.

Lloyd, M. (1996) A feminizt mapping of Foucauldian politics, in S. Hekman (ed.) *Feminist Interpretations of Michel Foucault*. University Park, PA: Pennsylvania Sate University Press.

Lucey, H., Brown, M., Denvir, H., Askew, M. and Rhodes, V. (2003) Girls and boys in the primary maths classroom, in C. Skelton and B. Francis (eds) *Boys and Girls in the Primary Classroom*. Maidenhead: Open University Press.

Mac an Ghaill, M. (1994) *The Making of Men: Masculinities, sexualities and schooling*. Buckingham: Open University Press.

Markus, T.A. (1993) *Buildings and Power: Freedom and control in the origin of modern building types*. London: Routledge.

Markus, T.A. (1996) Early nineteenth century school space and ideology, *Pedagogica Historica* 32(1): 9–50.

Marsh, J. (2000) 'But I want to fly too!': girls and superhero play in the infant classroom, *Gender and Education* 12(2): 209–20.

Martin, C.L., Ruble, D.N. and Szkrybalo, J. (2002) Cognitive theories of early gender development, *Psychological Bulletin* 128(6): 903–33.

Martin, R. (1988) Truth, power, self: an interview with Michel Foucault, in L.H. Martin, H. Gutman and P.H. Hutton (eds) *Technologies of the Self: A seminar with Michel Foucault*. Amherst, MA: University of Massachusetts Press.

Martino, W. and Meyenn, B. (2002) 'War, guns and cool, tough things': interrogating single-sex classes as a strategy for engaging boys in English, *Cambridge Journal of Education* 32(3): 303–24.

Martino, W. and Pallotta-Chiarolli, M. (2003) *So What's a Boy? Addressing issues of masculinity and schooling*. Maidenhead: Open University Press.

Martino, W., Lingard, B. and Mills, M. (2004) Issues in boys' education: a question of teacher threshold knowledges, *Gender and Education* 16(4): 435–54.

Mason-Schrock, D. (1996) Transsexuals' narrative construction of the 'true self', *Social Psychology Quarterly* 59(3): 176–92.

Massey, D. (1994) *Space, Place and Gender*. Cambridge: Polity Press.

Massey, D. (1995) Masculinity, dualisms and high technology, *Transactions of the Institute of British Geographers* 20(4): 487–99.

Massey, D. (1999) *Power-Geometries and the Politics of Space-time: Hettner-*

Lecture 1998. Heidelberg: Department of Geography, University of Heidelberg.

McFarlane, J. (1998) Looking through a glass darkly: a reading of Bronwyn Davies' *Shards of Glass: Children Reading and Writing beyond Gendered Identities*, *Women's Studies International Forum* 21(2): 199–208.

McGuffey, C.S. and Rich, B.L. (1999) Playing in the gender transgression zone: race, class and hegemonic masculinity in middle childhood, *Gender and Society* 13(5): 608–27.

McRobbie, A. (1991) *Feminism and Youth Culture*. Basingstoke: Macmillan Education.

McRobbie, A. (1996) *More!*: New sexualities in girls' and women's magazines, in J. Curran, D. Morley and V. Walkerdine (eds) *Cultural Studies and Communications*. London: Arnold.

Mendick, H. (2006) *Masculinities in Mathematics*. Buckingham: Open University Press.

Messner, M.A. (2000) Barbie girls versus sea monsters: children constructing gender, *Gender and Society* 14(6): 765–84.

Millard, E. (2005) To enter the castle of fear: engendering children's story writing from home to school at KS2, *Gender and Education* 17(1): 57–73.

Mills, M. (2001) Pushing it to the max: interrogating the risky business of being a boy, in W. Martino and B. Meyenn (eds) *What about the Boys? Issues of masculinity in schools*. Buckingham: Open University Press.

Mjelde, L. (2004) Changing work, changing households: new challenges to masculinity and femininity in Norwegian vocational education, in R.D. Lakes and P.A. Carter (eds) *Globalizing Education for Work: Comparative perspectives on gender and the new economy*. Mahwah, NJ: Lawrence Erlbaum.

Moi, T. (1999) *What Is a Woman?* Oxford: Oxford University Press.

Mondschein, E., Adolph, K.E. and Tamis-LeMonda, C.S. (2000) Gender bias in mothers' expectations about infant crawling, *Journal of Experimental Child Psychology* 77: 304–16.

Money, J. and Ehrhardt, A.A. (1972) *Man and Woman, Boy and Girl: The differentiation and dimorphism of gender identity from conception to maturity*. Baltimore, MD: Johns Hopkins University Press.

Morley, D. (1992) *Television Audiences and Cultural Studies*. London: Routledge.

Morley, D. (2000) *Home Territories: Media, mobility and identity*. London: Routledge.

Mort, F. and Peters, R. (2005) Foucault recalled: interview with Michel Foucault, *New Formations* 55: 9–22.

Moss, G. and Attar, D. (1999) Boys and literacy: gendering the reading curriculum, in J. Prosser (ed.) *School Culture*. London: Paul Chapman.

Münch, J. European Centre for the Development of Vocational Education (1995) *Vocational Education and Training in the Federal Republic of Germany*. Luxembourg: Office for Official Publications of the European Communities.

National Women's Law Center (2002) *Title IX and Equal Opportunity in Vocational and Technical Education: A promise still owed to the nation's young women*. Washington, DC: National Women's Law Center.

Nayak, A. and Kehily, M.J. (2001) 'Learning to laugh': a study of schoolboy humour, in W. Martino and B. Meyenn (eds) *What about the Boys? Issues of masculinity in schools*. Buckingham: Open University Press.

Nespor, J. (1997) *Tangled up in School*. Mahwah, NJ: Lawrence Erlbaum.

Nordenmark, M. and Nyman, C. (2003) Fair or unfair? Perceived fairness of household division of labour and gender equality among women and men: the Swedish case, *European Journal of Women's Studies* 10(2): 181–209.

O'Brien, J. (1999) Writing in the body: gender (re)production in online interaction, in M.A. Smith and P. Kollock (eds) *Communities in Cyberspace*. London: Routledge.

O'Donnell, M. and Sharpe, S. (2000). *Uncertain Masculinities: Youth, ethnicity and class in contemporary Britain*. London: Routledge.

Orbach, S. (1993) Heterosexuality and parenting, in S. Wilkinson and C. Kitzinger (eds) *Heterosexuality: A feminizm and psychology reader*. London: Sage.

O'Sullivan, M., Bush, K. and Gehring, M. (2002) Gender equity and physical education: a USA perspective, in D. Penney (ed.) *Gender and Physical Education: Contemporary issues and future directions*. London: Routledge.

Pae, H.K. and Lakes, R.D. (2004) Preparation for (in)equality: women in South Korea, in R.D. Lakes and P.A. Carter (eds) *Globalizing Education for Work: Comparative perspectives on gender and the new economy*. Mahwah, NJ: Lawrence Erlbaum.

Paechter, C. (1998) *Educating the Other: Gender, power and schooling*. London: Falmer Press.

Paechter, C. (1999) Issues in the study of curriculum in the context of lifelong learning. Paper presented to the British Educational Research Association, University of Sussex, September.

Paechter, C. (2000) *Changing School Subjects: Power, gender and curriculum*. Buckingham: Open University Press.

Paechter, C. (2003a) Learning masculinities and femininities: power/ knowledge and legitimate peripheral participation, *Women's Studies International Forum* 26(6): 541–52.

Paechter, C. (2003b) Masculinities and femininities as communities of practice, *Women's Studies International Forum* 26(1): 69–77.

Paechter, C. (2003c) Power, bodies and identity: how different forms of physical education construct varying masculinities and femininities in secondary schools, *Sex Education* 3(1): 47–59.

Paechter, C. (2004) 'Mens sana in corpore sano': Cartesian dualism and the marginalization of sex education, *Discourse* 25(3): 309–20.

Paechter, C. (2006a) Femininities and schooling, in C. Skelton, B. Francis and L. Smulyan (eds) *Handbook of Gender and Education*. London: Sage.

Paechter, C. (2006b) Power, knowledge and embodiment in communities of sex/gender practice, *Women's Studies International Forum* 29(1): 13–26.

Paechter, C. (2006c) Reconceptualizing the gendered body: learning and constructing masculinities and femininities in school, *Gender and Education* 18(2): 121–35.

Paechter, C. (2006d) Tomboy identities: The construction and maintenance of active girlhood. ESRC award RES-00-22-1032. Research report, Goldsmiths College, London.

Paechter, C. (2007) National curricula, in B.J. Bank, S. Delamont and C. Marshall (eds) *Gender and Education: an Encyclopedia*. New York, NY: Greenwood Press.

Parker, A. (1996) The construction of masculinity within boys' physical education, *Gender and Education* 8(2): 141–57.

Pascoe, C. J. (2007) *Dude, You're a Fag: Masculinity and sexuality in adolescence*. Berkeley, CA: University of California Press.

Patton, P. (1979) Of power and prisons, in M. Morris and P. Patton (eds) *Michel Foucault: Power, Truth, Strategy*. Sydney: Feral Publications.

Phillips, H. (2005) Conference report: neuroscience. *New Scientist* 2527 (26 November): 12–3.

Power, S., Edwards, T., Whitty, G. and Wigfall, V. (2003). *Education and the Middle Class*. Buckingham: Open University Press.

Pratt, S. and George, R. (2005) Transferring friendship: girls' and boys' friendships in the transition from primary to secondary school, *Children and Society* 19: 16–26.

Preves, S.E. (2003) *Intersex and Identity*. New Brunswick, NJ: Rutgers University Press.

Prosser, J. (1998) *Second Skins: The body narratives of transsexuality*. New York, NY: Columbia University Press.

Rapoport, T., Garb, Y. and Penso, A. (1995) Religious socialization and female subjectivity: religious-Zionist adolescent girls in Israel, *Sociology of Education* 68: 48–61.

Reay, D. (2001) 'Spice girls', 'nice girls', 'girlies' and 'tomboys': gender discourses, girls' cultures and femininities in the primary classroom, *Gender and Education* 13(2): 153–66.

Redman, P. (1996) 'Empowering men to disempower themselves': heterosexual masculinities, HIV and the contradictions of anti-oppressive education, in M. Mac an Ghaill (ed.) *Understanding Masculinities: Social relations and cultural arenas*. Buckingham: Open University Press.

Redman, P. (2001) The discipline of love: negotiation and regulation in boys' performance of romance-based heterosexual masculinity, *Men and Masculinities* 4(2): 186–200.

Redman, P. and Mac an Ghaill, M. (1997) Educating Peter: the making of a history man, in D. Steinberg and D. Epstein (eds) *Border Patrols: Policing the boundaries of heterosexuality*. London: Cassell.

Reichert, M.C. (2001) Rethinking masculinities: new ideas for schooling boys, in W. Martino and B. Meyenn (eds) *What about the Boys? Issues of masculinity in schools*. Buckingham: Open University Press.

Renold, E. (2001) 'Square-girls', femininity and the negotiation of academic success in the primary school, *British Educational Research Journal* 27(5): 577–88.

Renold, E. (2004) 'Other' boys: negotiating non-hegemonic masculinities in the primary school, *Gender and Education* 16(2): 247–66.

Renold, E. (2005) *Girls, Boys and Junior Sexualities: Exploring children's gender and sexual relations in the primary school*. London: Routledge.

Renold, E. and Allan, A. (2004) Bright and beautiful: high-achieving girls, ambivalent femininities and the feminization of success. Unpublished paper, University of Cardiff.

Rhedding-Jones, J. (2003) Reconceptualizing gender: new theorizations from early childhood education data. Paper presented to the British Educational Research Association Annual Conference, Edinburgh, September.

Richardson, H.H. (1981) *The Getting of Wisdom*. London: Virago. First published in 1910.

Robinson, T. (1994) Hard. *Love Over Rage*. Compact disc, Cooking Vinyl Ltd.

Ruble, D.N. and Martin, C.L. (1998) Gender development, in W. Damon and N. Eisenberg (eds) *Handbook of Child Psychology*. New York, NY: Wiley.

Russell, R. and Tyler, M. (2005) Branding and bricolage: gender, consumption and transition, *Childhood* 12(2): 221–37.

Sacks, O. (1993) Making up the mind. *New York Review of Books* (8 April): 42–7.

Salisbury, J. and Jackson, D. (1996) *Challenging Macho Values: Practical ways of working with adolescent boys*. London: Falmer Press.

Sanders, S.A.L. and Burke, H. (1994) Are you a lesbian, miss? in D. Epstein (ed.) *Challenging Lesbian and Gay Inequalities in Education*. Buckingham: Open University Press.

Scott, K.A. (2002) 'You want to be a girl and not my friend': African-American/Black girls' play activities, *Childhood* 9(4): 397–414.

Sewell, T. (1997) *Black Masculinities in Schooling: How Black boys survive modern schooling.* Stoke-on-Trent: Trentham Books.

Shain, F. (2003) *The Schooling and Identity of Asian Girls.* Stoke-on-Trent: Trentham Books.

Shakib, S. and Dunbar, M. (2002) The social construction of female and male high school basketball participation: reproducing the gender order through a two-tiered sporting institution, *Sociological Perspectives* 45(4): 353–78.

Shilling, C. (1992) Schooling and the production of physical capital, *Discourse* 13(1): 1–19.

Simpson, H. (2001a) *Dear George.* London: Vintage.

Simpson, H. (2001b) *Hey Yeah Right Get a Life.* London: Vintage.

Skeggs, B. (1997) *Formations of Class and Gender.* London: Sage.

Skelton, C. (2001) *Schooling the Boys: Masculinities and primary education.* Buckingham: Open University Press.

Skelton, C. (2002) The 'feminization of schooling' or 'remasculizing' primary education?, *International Studies on the Sociology of Education* 12(1): 77–96.

Skelton, C. and Francis, B. (2003) Introduction: Boys and girls in the primary classroom, in C. Skelton and B. Francis (eds) *Boys and Girls in the Primary Classroom.* Maidenhead: Open University Press.

Skelton, C. and Hall, E. (2001) *The Development of Gender Roles in Young Children: A review of policy and literature.* Manchester: Equal Opportunities Commission.

Smith, C. and Lloyd, B. (1978) Maternal behaviour and perceived sex of infant: revisited, *Child Development* 49: 1263–5.

Smith, P.K., Cowie, H. and Blades, M. (1998) *Understanding Child Development.* Oxford: Basil Blackwell.

Spark, M. (1961) *The Prime of Miss Jean Brodie.* London: Penguin.

Sparkes, A.C. (1994) Self, silence and invisibility as a beginning teacher: a life history of lesbian experience, *British Journal of Sociology of Education* 15(1): 93–118.

Stern, D.N. (1991) *Diary of a Baby.* London: Fontana.

Stern, M. and Karraker, K.H. (1989) Sex stereotyping of infants: a review of gender labelling, *Sex Roles* 20(9/10): 501–22.

Stoller, R.J. (1968) *Sex and Gender: On the development of masculinity and femininity.* New York, NY: Science House.

Sullivan, C. (1993) Oppression: the experiences of a lesbian teacher in an inner city comprehensive school in the United Kingdom, *Gender and Education* 5(1): 93–101.

Swain, J. (2000) 'The money's good, the fame's good, the girls are good':

the role of playground football in the construction of young boys' masculinity in a junior school, *British Journal of Sociology of Education* 21(1): 95–109.

Swain, J. (2003) How young schoolboys become some*body*: the role of the body in the construction of masculinity, *British Journal of Sociology of Education* 24(3): 299–314.

Swain, J. (2005) Sharing the same world: boys' relations with girls during their last year of primary school, *Gender and Education* 17(1): 75–91.

Theberge, N. (2003) 'No fear comes': Adolescent girls, ice hockey and the embodiment of gender, *Youth and Society* 34(4): 497–516.

Thorne, B. (1993) *Gender Play: Girls and boys in school*. Buckingham: Open University Press.

Tolman, D.L., Spencer, R., Harman, T., Rosen-Reynose, M. and Striepe, M. (2004) Getting close, staying cool: early adolescent boys' experiences with romantic relationships, in N. Way and J.Y. Chu (eds) *Adolescent Boys: Exploring diverse cultures of boyhood*. New York, NY: New York University Press.

Turnbull, A. (1987) Learning her womanly work: the elementary school curriculum 1870–1914, in F. Hunt (ed.) *Lessons for Life*. Oxford: Basil Blackwell.

Udry, J.R. (2000) Biological limits of gender construction, *American Sociological Review* 65: 443–57.

Valentine, G. (1997) 'My son's a bit dizzy'. 'My wife's a bit soft': Gender, children and cultures of parenting, *Gender, Place and Culture* 4(1): 37–62.

Waerdahl, R. (2005) 'Maybe I'll need a pair of Levi's before Junior High?' Child to youth trajectories and anticipatory socialization, *Childhood* 12(2): 201–19.

Walden, R. and Walkerdine, V. (1985) *Girls and Mathematics: From primary to secondary schooling*. London: Heinemann.

Walkerdine, V. (1984) Developmental psychology and the child-centred pedagogy: the insertion of Piaget into early education, in J. Henriques, W. Hollway, C. Urwin, C. Venn and V. Walkerdine (eds) *Changing the Subject*. London: Methuen.

Walkerdine, V. (1988) *The Mastery of Reason*. London: Routledge & Kegan Paul.

Walkerdine, V. and The Girls and Mathematics Unit (1989) *Counting Girls Out*. London: Virago.

Walkerdine, V., Lucey, H. and Melody, J. (2001) *Growing Up Girl: Psychosocial explorations of gender and class*. Basingstoke: Palgrave.

Warin, J. (2000) The attainment of self-consistency through gender in young children, *Sex Roles* 42(3/4): 209–31.

Warrington, M., Younger, M. and McLellan, R. (2003) 'Underachieving boys' in English primary schools?, *Curriculum Journal* 14(2): 139–56.

Way, N. (2004) Intimacy, desire, and distrust in the friendships of adolescent boys, in N. Way and J.Y. Chu (eds) *Adolescent Boys: Exploring diverse cultures of boyhood*. New York, NY: New York University Press.

Weekes, D. (2004) Where my girls at? Black girls and the construction of the sexual, in A. Harris (ed.) *All about the Girl: Culture, power and identity*. London: Routledge.

Wenger, E. (1998) *Communities of Practice: Learning, meaning and identity*. Cambridge: Cambridge University Press.

West, C. and Zimmerman, D.H. (1987) Doing gender, *Gender and Society* 1(2): 125–51.

Wilans, G. and Searle, R. (1958) *Down with Skool!* London: May Fair Books.

Wilder, L. I. (1992) On the banks of Plum Creek. In *The Complete Little House on the Prarie*. London: Methuen.

Wille, D.E. (1995) The 1990s: Gender differences in parenting roles, *Sex Roles* 33(11/12): 803–17.

Williams, A. (1993) Who cares about girls? Equality, physical education and the primary school child, in J. Evans (ed.) *Equality, Education and Physical Education*. London: Falmer Press.

Williams, A. and Bedward, J. (1999) A more inclusive curriculum framework (QCA 1999) – making physical education more relevant to adolescent girls, *British Journal of Physical Education* 30(3): 6–10.

Williams, A. and Bedward, J. (2002) Understanding girls' experience of physical education: relational analysis and situated learning, in D. Penney (ed.) *Gender and Physical Education: Contemporary issues and future directions*. London: Routledge.

Williams, L.S. (2002) Trying on gender, gender regimes, and the processes of becoming women, *Gender and Society* 16(1): 29–52.

Willis, P. (1977). *Learning to Labour*. Aldershot: Gower.

Woodward, D. (2003) Nursery class children's formation of gender perspectives. Unpublished MPhil thesis, Faculty of Education and Language Studies, Open University, Milton Keynes.

Woolf, V. (1977). *The Waves*. St. Albans: Panther. First published in 1931.

Xiao, H. (2000) Class, gender, and parental values in the 1990s, *Gender and Society* 14(6): 785–803.

Youdell, D. (2005) Sex-gender-sexuality: how sex, gender and sexuality constellations are constituted in secondary schools, *Gender and Education* 17(3): 249–70.

Young, I.M. (2005) *On Female Body Experience: 'Throwing like a girl' and other essays*. Oxford: Oxford University Press.

Index